Conversational
GERMAN
in 7 Days

WITHDRAWN

---

*Master Language Survival Skills
in Just One Week!*

Shirley Baldwin and Sarah Boas

McGraw·Hill

New York   Chicago   San Francisco   Lisbon   London   Madrid   Mexico City
Milan   New Delhi   San Juan   Seoul   Singapore   Sydney   Toronto

Originally published by Hodder & Stoughton Publishers.

5 6 7 8 9 0   WKT/WKT   2 1 0 9 8 7

ISBN 0-07-143261-2 (package)
      0-07-143260-4 (book)

Acknowledgments
The authors and publishers are grateful to the following for supplying photographs:
Barnaby's Picture Library (pp. 14, 74)
J. Allan Cash Ltd. (pp. 1, 5, 10, 12, 13, 18, 21, 22, 25, 30, 31, 33, 34, 35, 38, 45, 48, 49, 50, 53, 57, 60, 64, 74)
The German Tourist Board (p. 70)

McGraw-Hill books are available at special quantity discounts to use as premiums and sales promotions, or for use in corporate training programs. For more information, please write to the Director of Special Sales, Professional Publishing, McGraw-Hill, Two Penn Plaza, New York, NY 10121-2298. Or contact your local bookstore.

This book is printed on acid-free paper.

Contents

INTRODUCTION

Conversational German in 7 Days is a short course that will equip you to deal with everyday situations when you visit a German-speaking country.

The course is divided into 7 units, each corresponding to a day in the life of George Jackson (a salesman) and his daughter Helen during their week in Germany. Each unit begins with a dialogue, which introduces the essential vocabulary in context. The phrasebook section lists these and other useful phrases and defines them in English. Within the units there are also sections giving basic grammatical explanations and a number of practice activities designed to be useful as well as fun. Answers can be checked in the back of the book. Also available with this program are 2 CDs to help you practice your German.

A note about the currency used in this book. In 2002, 12 countries in the European Union, including Germany and Austria, adopted the Euro as the national currency. The official currency of Switzerland remains the Swiss franc. In this book, the dialogues and text refer to the former currency of Germany, the *Deutsche Mark*.

Pronunciation

Remember to pronounce every sound in a German word, even the final **-e**.

Consonants: similar to English, but:

German sound	example
ch as in *loch*:	Tochter [tochter]
j as in *yet*:	jetzt [yetst]
qu as in *kvass*:	Quelle [kveller]
s z (+ a vowel):	sind [zind]
otherwise as *s*:	ist [ist]
ß as *s*:	naß [nahss]
sch as in *shop*:	schon [shown]
sp *shp* (at the beginning):	spät [shpate]
st *sht* (at the beginning):	Stadt [shtat]
v as in *fat*:	vier [fear]
w as in *vain*:	wie [vee]
z as in *lots*:	Zimmer [tsimmer]
-b, -d at the end of a word: *p, t*	
-ig at the end of a word: *ich*	
r trilled or rolled at beginning, always sounded at end: rot [rote] Herr [hair]	

Vowels: similar to English:

German sound	example
a long, as *father*	Tag [tark]
a short, as *Bach*	danke [danker]
e long, as *day*	leben [layben]
e short, as *net*	es [ess]
i as in *pin*	ich [ich]
i as in *beet*	ihn [een]
o long, as *so*	Brot [brote]
o short, as *pot*	komm [kom]
u long, as *boot*	gut [goot]
u short, as *put*	Mutti [mooti]
ie as in *keep*	hier [here]

Vowels with an umlaut

ä long, as *fate*	spät [shpate]
ä short, as *met*	Pässe [pesser]
ö sim. French *œil*	Öl [erl]
ü, y sim. Fr. *une*	früh [frew]
äu as in *boy*	läuft [loyft]

Dipthongs

au as in *town*	Haus [house]
eu as in *boy*	neu [noy]
ei, ai as in *fine*	mein [mein]

INTRODUCTIONS AND GREETINGS

▶ **Arrival** When arriving at a port or airport, you will find customs and passport procedures standard and easy to follow, as most information is given in English as well as German. You should check your duty-free allowance before setting out on your journey. Look out for these signs: **ZOLL** (Customs), **PASSKONTROLLE** (passport check), and when crossing the border—**GRENZE** (frontier).

am Flughafen/at the airport

George Jackson and his daughter Helen (17), a student, arrive at the airport. George, a sports equipment salesman, is met by a German colleague, Ernst Fischer, while Helen is greeted by the Bauer family with whom she is staying as a boarder.

Ernst:	Entschuldigen Sie, bitte. **Sind Sie** Herr Jackson?
George:	Ja, **mein Name ist** Jackson. Und sind Sie Herr Fischer?
Ernst:	Ja, **ich heiße** Ernst Fischer. Also, **sehr erfreut**, Herr Jackson.
Ulrike:	(approaching) **Guten Tag**—sind Sie Fräulein Helen Jackson? **Ich bin** Ulrike Bauer, und **das ist** Gisela, meine Tochter.
Gisela:	Guten Tag. **Wie geht's?**
Helen:	**Gut, danke.**

Ulrike:	Aha, hier ist Thomas. Er kommt immer zu spät.
Gisela:	(to Helen) Das ist mein Bruder, Thomas
Ernst:	Hier ist unser Taxi, Herr Jackson. Geben Sie mir das Gepäck. (To the driver) Hotel Berlin, bitte.
Ulrike:	Thomas, ist das Auto da?
Thomas:	Ja, Mutti.
Ulrike:	Helen, ist das Ihre Reisetasche? Wo ist Ihr Koffer? Wir fahren jetzt nach Hause.

Father and daughter say goodbye to each other and arrange to meet soon.

Ulrike:	**Auf Wiedersehen**, Herr Jackson.
George:	Auf Wiedersehen, Frau Bauer.

Saying hello and goodbye It is customary to *shake hands* when greeting people in German-speaking countries, and to say good day and goodbye on entering and leaving such places as shops and restaurants. In Southern Germany and Austria, ''Grüß* Gott'' is used instead of ''Guten Tag.'' Address a man as **Herr** Jackson, most women as **Frau** Bauer, a girl or very young unmarried woman as **Fräulein** Bauer. Unlike in other languages, **Herr, Frau** and **Fräulein** are not used on their own.
*Note that the German letter ß is pronounced as an ''s.''

Introductions

Entschuldigen Sie, bitte.	Excuse me, please.
Verzeihen Sie.	Pardon, excuse me.
Sind Sie Herr/Frau/Fräulein . . . ?	Are you Mr/Mrs/Miss. . . . ?
Ja/Nein	Yes/No
Wie ist Ihr Name?/Wie heißen Sie?	What is your name?
Ihr Name, bitte.	Your name, please.
Mein Name ist . . ./Ich heiße . . .	My name is . . .
Ich bin . . .	I am . . .
Sehr erfreut.	Pleased to meet you.

Greetings and farewells

Guten Tag.	Hello/Good day.
Guten Morgen.	Good morning.
Guten Abend.	Good evening.
Gute Nacht.	Good night.
Hallo.	Hello.
Wie geht es Ihnen?	How are you?
Wie geht's?	How are things?
Gut, danke	Fine, thanks
Und Ihnen?	And you?
Auf Wiedersehen.	Goodbye.
Bis bald.	See you later.

Wie geht's? Gut, danke

Please and thank you

Bitte/Ja, bitte.	Please/Yes, please.
Danke.	Thank you (can mean "no thank you").
Vielen Dank/Danke schön.	Many thanks/Thank you very much.
Bitte schön.	Don't mention it/You're welcome.

USEFUL WORDS AND EXPRESSIONS

und/also!	and/well then!
das ist meine Tochter	that's my daughter
Er kommt immer zu spät.	He's always too late.
mein Bruder	my brother
Hier ist unser Taxi/das Auto.	Here's our taxi/the car.
Geben Sie mir das Gepäck.	Give me your luggage.
da	there
Ja, Mutti.	Yes, Mom.
Wo ist Ihr Koffer?	Where is your suitcase?
Ihre Reisetasche	your travel bag
Wir fahren jetzt nach Hause.	We're going home now.

the way it works

The

All nouns in German begin with a capital letter:

meine **T**ochter   my daughter   das **A**uto   the car

The word for "the" in German varies according to whether the noun is masculine, feminine or neuter.

For a masculine noun, use **der**:   **der** Koffer   the suitcase
For a feminine noun, use **die**:   **die** Reisetasche   the travel bag
For a neuter noun, use **das**:   **das** Gepäck   the luggage

Sometimes it is possible to guess whether a noun is masculine or feminine: e.g., **der Bruder** (the brother), **die Mutter** (the mother); but in general, each noun must be learned together with its gender.

My and your

These are adjectives, and in German they vary depending on whether the noun is masculine, feminine, or neuter.

For a masculine noun, say: **mein Name**   my name,   **Ihr Name**   your name
For a feminine noun, say: **meine Tochter**   my daughter,   **Ihre Tochter** your daughter
For a neuter noun, say: **mein Auto**   my car,   **Ihr Auto**   your car

Note that **Ihr** is always written with a capital letter. Note also **unser, unsere** (our).

I, you and he (pronouns)

In German, these are **ich**, **Sie**, and **er**. **Sie** is always written with a capital letter. In the dialogue, these pronouns are used with the verb "to be" as follows:

ich bin   I am   **Sie sind**   you are   **er ist**   he is

3

Asking questions

If you want to ask a question in German, you simply turn the sentence around, as in English:

Sie sind Herr Jackson.   You are Mr. Jackson.   Da ist das Auto.   There is the car.
Sind Sie Herr Jackson?   Are you Mr. Jackson?   Ist das Auto da?   Is the car there?

things to do

1.1 A tour guide is meeting the train at the station, and asks the following passengers if they are members of his group. Reply for them, using complete sentences.

1   John Lowe—Entschuldigen Sie bitte, sind Sie Herr Lowe?
2   Françoise Leclerc—Sind Sie Fräulein Dupont?
3   Kirk Tyler—Entschuldigen Sie bitte, heißen Sie Kennedy?
4   José Garcia—Entschuldigen Sie bitte, sind Sie Herr Garcia?
5   Rosemary Brown—Heißen Sie Baker?

Now he tells them his own name. What does he say?

1.2 Practice greeting the following people:

1   Herr Schneider: Say hello and ask him how things are.
2   Frau Schwarz: Say good morning.
3   Herr Kohl: Say good evening, and tell him you are pleased to meet him.
4   Fräulein Schmidt: Say good day, and ask her how she is.

1.3 Die Familie *The family*

DIE ELTERN (The parents)
der Mann (husband)
der Vater (father)

die Frau (wife)
die Mutter (Mother)

Ludwig   Ulrike

DIE KINDER (the children)
der Sohn (son)
der Bruder (brother)

die Tochter (daughter)
die Schwester (sister)

Thomas 19   Gisela 16

Imagine you are Karl-Heinrich Bauer, and you are explaining your relationship to other members of your family. What would you say? The first one is done for you.

1   Ludwig ist mein Vater.   3   Thomas . . . .
2   Ulrike ist   4   Gisela . . . .

Now Ludwig begins to point out the members of his family, beginning: **Das ist Ulrike, meine Frau.** But Ulrike continues with the explanation. What does she say about Ludwig, Thomas, Gisela and Karl-Heinrich?

MAKING A HOTEL RESERVATION

Accommodations   There are many different types and categories of hotel,
varying from the very basic to the luxurious, with facilities such as saunas,
fitness centers and swimming pools. Detailed lists can be obtained from the
German, Austrian and Swiss National Tourist Offices. Booking in advance is
advisable, especially in the summer, and you normally pay for the room
rather than per person. You will be expected to fill out a registration form
giving details of nationality, occupation, passport number, etc.
A few types of accommodations are: **Hotel garni** (bed and breakfast);
Pension (boarding house); **Gasthaus/Gasthof** (country inn);
Ferienwohnung/Appartements (vacation apartments).
When traveling through the countryside, look for the sign **ZIMMER FREI**
(rooms available) by the roadside, or go to the nearest
Fremdenverkehrsbüro (tourist office), which will keep a list of hotels and
other accommodations. In Germany, hotels and apartments may be located
in castles, stately homes and historic inns (details from the GNTO) and
vacations can be taken at farmhouses. There are over 600 **Jugendherbergen**
(youth hostels) for members of the International Youth Hostels Association.

Prices

Wieviel kostet das Zimmer?	How much is the room?
pro Nacht	per night
Es kostet zweihundertfünfzig Mark pro Tag.	It costs DM 250 a day.
Einzelzimmer Zuschlag, DM, 10,–	Single room surcharge, 10 Marks
Das ist zu teuer.	That's too much.
Haben Sie etwas Billigeres?	Have you anything cheaper?
Ich nehme es.	I'll take it.
Wollen Sie sich bitte eintragen?	Please register.
Hier ist die Bestätigung.	Here is the confirmation.
Zimmer acht, im Erdgeschoß	Room 8, on the ground floor
Hier ist der Schlüssel.	Here is the key.
die Mehrwertsteuer.	sales tax.
Es tut mir leid.	I'm sorry.
Es ist kein Zimmer frei.	We have no room.

MAKING CONVERSATION

zu Hause/in the house

Helen Jackson is talking to Ludwig, Gisela and Thomas's father.

Ludwig: England ist sehr schön, aber das Wetter ist nicht gut! Sie wohnen in Manchester, Helen, nicht wahr?

Helen: Nein, ich wohne nicht in Manchester. **Ich wohne in London. Ich bin Londonerin.**

Ludwig: Ah, Sie sind Londonerin! Ich habe eine Kusine in London. Und Sie sind sechzehn Jahre, alt. Wie Gisela?

Gisela: (entering) Nein, Vati, sie ist siebzehn…Komm Helen, das Abendessen ist nun bereit.

Where are you from?

Woher kommen Sie?	Where do you come from?
Woher sind Sie?	Where are you from?
Ich komme aus Amerika/Deutschland/ Österreich.	I come from America/Germany/Austria.
Ich bin aus der Schweiz/aus Amerika.	I'm from Switzerland/America.
Wo wohnen Sie?	Where do you live?
Ich wohne in New York/München/Wien.	I live in New York/Munich/Vienna
Ich bin New Yorker/New Yorkerin.	I am a New Yorker (male/female).

How old are you?
(For a list of numbers, see p. 77)

Wie alt sind Sie?	How old are you?
Ich bin neunzehn Jahre alt.	I am nineteen years old.

USEFUL WORDS AND EXPRESSIONS

(Einen) Moment, bitte.	Just a moment, please.	**Ich habe eine Kusine in London.**	I have a cousin in London.
das stimmt	that's right		
aber	but	**Komm**	Come (along)
nicht wahr?	don't you? (etc.)	**Vati**	Dad
England ist sehr schön.	England is very nice.	**das Abendessen**	supper
		nun	now
Das Wetter ist nicht gut.	The weather is not good.	**bereit**	ready

the way it works

a and an

In the same way as "my" and "your," the word for "a"/"an" is different, depending whether the noun is masculine, feminine or neuter.

For a masculine noun, use **ein**: **ein** Schlüssel
For a feminine noun, use **eine**: **eine** Woche
For a neuter noun, use **ein**: **ein** Zimmer

More pronouns

"She" is **sie**: "we" is **wir**.

sie ist siebzehn she is seventeen
wir haben Zimmer frei we have rooms available

Here is a list of the pronouns in German, used with the verb **sein** (to be):

ich bin	I am	**wir sind**	we are
du bist	you are (informal)	**Sie sind**	you are (plural)
Sie sind	you are (formal)	**sie sind**	they are
er ist	he is		
sie ist	she is		
es ist	it is		

Verbs

Two more verbs used in this unit are **kommen** (to come) and **wohnen** (to live). Many other German verbs form their endings in the same way as these:

ich **komme**	I come	wir **kommen**	we come
du **kommst**	you come	Sie **kommen**	you come (pl)
Sie **kommen**	you come	sie **kommen**	they come
er/sie/es **kommt**	he/she/it comes		

The verb **haben** (to have) is irregular, and should be learned:

ich **habe**	I have	wir **haben**	we have
du **hast**	you have	Sie **haben**	you have (pl)
Sie **haben**	you have	sie **haben**	they have
er/sie/es **hat**	he/she/it has		

Negatives

To make a sentence negative, simply use **nicht**:

Das Wetter ist **nicht** gut. The weather is not good.
Sind Sie **nicht** aus Boston? Aren't you from Boston?
Ich wohne **nicht** in Dallas. I don't live in Dallas.

things to do

1.4 *Reserving a hotel room*
Practice making a room reservation. Use **Ich möchte** (I would like):

1

2

3

4

5

1.5 The hotel receptionist is looking at the wrong day in the register and has become confused. Can you correct her?

1.6 The following people are on vacation abroad. Can you tell from their car nationality plates where they come from? The first one is done for you.

1 Ulrike Bauer **D**   Sie kommt aus Deutschland.

2 George Jackson **GB**

3 Andreas Mueller **CH**

4 Fritz Stern **Ö**

5 Amy Krupnik **USA**

1.7 Wie alt sind sie? *(How old are they?)*
Practice using numbers in German by saying how old these people are. The first one is done for you.

1 Gisela Bauer (16)
 Sie ist sechzehn.
2 Peter Böhm (12).
3 Margit Springer (5).

4 Günther Mayer (14).
5 Tomas Springer (7).
6 Ursula Böhm (20).

ORDERING BREAKFAST

▶▶▶ **Breakfast**   This is traditionally a fairly substantial meal, and will often consist of boiled eggs, cold cuts and sliced cheese as well as bread and rolls. In larger hotels, you may also be offered **muesli** (similar to granola) and yogurt. Coffee comes with cream, and you will have to ask for fresh milk (**frisches Milch**). Breakfast is usually served from 7 to 10 a.m. in hotels.

das Frühstück/breakfast

George Jackson is ordering breakfast at the hotel.

George: **Ich möchte frühstücken**, bitte.
Kellner: Was nehmen Sie? Es gibt Spiegeleier mit Speck, gekochte Eier, Rühreier, Schinken, Käse . . .
George: **Bringen Sie mir bitte Toast, mit Marmelade, und ein Glas Orangensaft.**
Kellner: Ja, gerne. Trinken Sie Tee oder Kaffee?
George: **Haben Sie heiße Schokolade?**
Kellner: Nein, wir haben keine Schokolade.
George: Also, **eine Tasse Kaffee—ohne Sahne**, bitte.
Kellner: Sonst noch etwas?
George: Nein danke. **Das ist alles**. Ich muß Diät leben!

What's for breakfast?

der Kellner/die Kellnerin	waiter/waitress
Ich möchte frühstücken.	I'd like to have breakfast.
Was nehmen Sie?	What will you have?
Was wollen Sie?	What do you want?
Was möchten Sie?	What would you like?
Es gibt . . .	There is/there are . . .
Wir haben . . .	We have . . .
Bringen Sie mir . . .	Bring me . . .
Spiegeleier mit Speck	fried eggs and bacon
gekochte Eier/ein gekochtes Ei	boiled eggs/a boiled egg
Rühreier/Schinken/Käse	scrambled eggs/ham/cheese
Joghurt/Wurst	yogurt/sausage
Brot/Schwarzbrot	bread/rye bread
Brötchen/Semmeln	rolls
(ein Stück) Toast	(a piece of) toast
mit Butter und Marmelade	with butter and jam
mit Apfelsinenmarmelade/Honig	with marmalade/honey
ein Glas Orangensaft	a glass of orange juice
ein Glas Grapefruitsaft	a glass of grapefruit juice
Trinken Sie Tee oder Kaffee?	Do you want tea or coffee?
Ich möchte . . .	I would like . . .
eine Tasse Tee	a cup of tea
mit Zitrone/mit Milch	with lemon/milk
ein Kännchen Kaffee	a pot of coffee
einen schwarzen Kaffe	a black coffee
eine Tasse Kaffee mit Sahne/	a cup of coffee with cream/
ohne Sahne	without cream
eine Tasse heiße Schokolade	a cup of hot chocolate
eine Tasse Mokka	a cup of mocha coffee
Wir haben keine heiße Schokolade.	We don't have any hot chocolate.
Sonst noch etwas?	Anything else?
Noch ein . . . , bitte.	Another . . . , please.
Das ist alles.	That's all.
Ich muß Diät leben.	I'm on a diet.

SHOPPING FOR FOOD AND CLOTHES

▶▶ **Shopping hours** Stores are open from 8 or 9 a.m. until 6:30 p.m., Monday through Friday, and until 1:30 p.m. on Saturdays (Germany and Austria). In Germany, shops are open later on the first Saturday of each month. In small towns, they may close for lunch between 1 and 3 p.m., though department stores will remain open. In Switzerland, stores close for half a day each week. In some places, bakeries are open on Sundays from 10 a.m. to noon and sell many different varieties of bread—black, wheat and white. Rye bread is popular, and wheat bread is more common than white.

verkaufen/shopping

Gisela Bauer wants to spend the morning shopping.

Gisela: Fahren wir heute morgen in die Stadt, Helen. Wir haben sehr schöne Geschäfte hier in München, und **ich suche einen Rock** für eine Party am Donnerstag.

Ulrike: Vergessen Sie nicht meine Einkäufe. (Reads from list) **Ich brauche Butter**, Käse, Reis, eine Dose Sardinen, Würstchen, zwei Kilo Zwiebeln, rote Bohnen, Äpfel, Pfirsiche, ein Dutzend Eier, eine Flasche Cola . . .

Gisela: Mutti, Mutti! Wir haben nicht soviel Zeit.

Ulrike: Du findest alles im Supermarkt, meine liebe Tochter. Hier Helen, nehmen Sie die Liste.

im Kaufhaus/at the department store

Gisela and Helen arrive at the third shop that morning.

Verkäuferin: Guten Morgen. Kann ich Ihnen helfen?

Gisela: Bitte, **wieviel kostet dieser Rock? Ich trage Größe 36.**

Verkäuferin: Der blaue Rock? Es tut mir leid. Wir haben nur Größe 38 oder 40.

Helen: Wie schade! Diese Kleider sind auch schön, Gisela.

Gisela: Die grünen? Ja, aber sie sind zu teuer und zu groß. (To the clerk) **Haben Sie nichts Kleineres und Billigeres** in blau?

Verfäuferin: Es tut mir leid.

Helen: Du bist so schlank! (Looking at her watch) Es ist spät; ich habe Hunger. Gibt es ein Restaurant im Kaufhaus?

Gisela: Nein, wir treffen meinen Bruder Thomas im Café. Aber zuerst zum Supermarkt!

Shopping for food

Einkäufe machen	to go shopping
Ich brauche . . .	I need . . .
Würstchen	little sausages
zwei Kilo Zwiebeln	2 kilos of onions
Äpfel, Pfirsiche	apples, peaches
ein Dutzend Eier	a dozen eggs
eine Flasche Cola	a bottle of cola

die Butter	butter	der Reis	rice
der Käse	cheese	der Zucker	sugar
die Margarine	margarine	das Mehl	flour
das Speiseöl	cooking oil	die Kekse	cookies
der Joghurt	yogurt	die Teigwaren	pasta
das Ei	egg	der Bohnenkaffee	(ground) coffee

Use the following expressions when buying food:

ein Stück Kuchen	a piece of cake
eine Packung Kekse	a bag of cookies
ein Paket Zucker	a bag of sugar
eine Packung Tee	a bag of tea
eine Dose Sardinen	a can of sardines
eine Packung Eier	a carton of eggs
eine Scheibe Schinken	a slice of ham
sechs Scheiben Salami	6 slices of salami
eine Schachtel Pralinen	a box of chocolates
eine Tafel Schokolade	a bar of chocolate
ein Brot	a loaf of bread

Measurements Don't forget that the metric system of weights and measures is used in Europe:

100 grams = 3.5 oz.	1 mile = 1.6 kilometers
1 kilogram = 2.2 lb	8 kilometers = 1 mile
1 liter = 1.06 qt.	

ein Kilo Birnen	a kilo of pears
ein halbes Kilo Äpfel	half a kilo of apples
zwei Kilo Kartoffeln	2 kilos of potatoes
ein Pfund Karotten	a pound of carrots
ein halbes Pfund Tomaten	half a pound of tomatoes
Hundert Gramm Käse	100 grams of cheese
Hundertfünfzig Gramm Leberwurst	150 grams of liver paté
ein Liter Milch	a liter of milk
eine Flasche Essig	a bottle of vinegar
Wieviel kostet . . . ?	How much does . . . cost?
Es kostet . . .DM pro Dutzend/per Kilo.	It costs . . . Marks a dozen/kilo.

Die Geschäfte (shops)

das Geschäft	store
der Markt	market
der Supermarkt	supermarket
das Einkaufszentrum	shopping center
das Kaufhaus/	
Warenhaus	department store

Here are some common shops:

die Bäckerei	bakery
das Lebensmittel-	
geschäft	grocery store
die Fleischerei/die	
Metzgerei	butcher shop
die Fischhandlung	fish market
die Obst und	
Gemüsehandlung	produce store
die Konditorei	cake shop, café
die Milchhandlung	dairy
das Delikatessen-	
geschäft	delicatessen
das Reformhaus	health food store

die Apotheke	pharmacy
die Drogerie	drugstore
der Zeitungshändler	newsstand
das Schreibwaren-	
geschäft	stationer's
die Buchhandlung	bookstore
das Modengeschäft	dress store
das Schuhgeschäft	shoe store
der Damenfriseur/	ladies/men's
Herrenfriseur	hairdresser
die chemische	dry cleaner's
Reinigung	

Look out for these notices:

SELBSTBEDIENUNG	self-service
KASSE	check-out
SCHNELLKASSE	express check-out

EINGANG	entrance
AUSGANG	exit
KEIN AUSGANG	no exit

Buying clothes

Kann ich Ihnen helfen?	Can I help you?
Was darf es sein?	What would you like?
Ich sehe mich nur um.	I'm just looking.
Ich suche . . .	I'm looking for . . .
Verkaufen Sie . . . ?	Do you sell . . . ?
Ich möchte . . . kaufen	I'd like to buy . . .

For a full list of clothes and colors, see p. 78)

Size and price

Zeigen Sie mir bitte . . .	Could you show me . . .
Welche Größe?	What size?
Ich trage/habe Größe 36	I wear size 8
Können Sie bitte meine Maße nehmen?	Can you measure me, please?
Es tut mir leid . . .	I'm sorry . . .
Wir haben keine . . . in dieser Größe.	We have no . . . in this size.
Wir haben nur Größe 38 oder 40.	We only have size 4 or 6.
Wieviel kostet dieser Rock?	How much does this skirt cost?
Es is zu teuer/groß/lang/kurz/klein/ eng.	It's too expensive/big/long/short/small tight.
Haben Sie nichts Kleineres/Billigeres?	Haven't you anything smaller/cheaper?
teuer/billig/preiswert	expensive/cheap/good value

Sizes

Women's dresses

American		4	6	8	10	12	14	16
European		38	40	42	44	46	48	50

Shoes

American	6	7	8	9	10	11	12	13
European	36	37	38	39	40	41	42	43

Collar sizes

American	14	14½	15	15½	16	16½	17
European	36	37	38	39–40	41	42	43

Decisions

Diese Kleider sind auch schön.	These dresses are nice too.
Ich habe die Farbe nicht gern.	I don't like the color.
Ich habe lieber blau/grün.	I prefer blue/green.
Kann ich es anprobieren?	Can I try it on?
Das gefällt mir nicht.	I don't like it.
Es paßt Ihnen ausgezeichnet.	It fits you perfectly.
Ich nehme es.	I'll take it.
Sonst noch einen Wunsch?	Would you like anything else?
Kann ich eine Quittung haben?	Can I have a receipt?

USEFUL WORDS AND EXPRESSIONS

Ja, gerne.	Yes, certainly.
Heute morgen	this morning
Fahren wir in die Stadt.	Let's go into town.
Wir haben sehr schöne Geschäfte.	We have very nice stores.
für eine Party	for a party
Vergessen Sie nicht . . .	Don't forget . . .
Wir haben nicht soviel Zeit.	We don't have much time.
Du findest alles im Supermarkt.	You'll find everything in the supermarket.
meine liebe Tochter	my dear daughter
Nehmen Sie die Liste.	Take the list.
Wie schade!	What a shame!
Du bist so schlank!	You are so slim!
Es ist spät.	It's late.
Ich habe Hunger.	I'm hungry.
Wir treffen meinen Bruder im Café.	We're meeting my brother at the café.
Zuerst zum Supermarkt!	First, to the supermarket!

the way it works

Du

Du also means "you" in German, but it is not used very often—only when talking to someone you know very well, children or members of the family:

Du findest alles im Supermarkt.	You find everything in the supermarket.
Du bist schlank.	You are slim.

Dein is the familiar form of "your," and works like **ein** and **mein**.

Nouns in the plural

"The' in the plural is **die**. Feminine nouns in the plural often take the ending **-n** or **-en**:

eine Bluse   zwei Bluse**n**   die Rechnung   die Rechnung**en**

Masculine and neuter nouns ending in **-el, -er** and **-en** often remain the same:

der Koffer	die Koffer	das Zimmer	die Zimmer
der Schlüssel	die Schlüssel	das Kissen	die Kissen

Others add an **-e**, or add an umlaut as well as an **-e**:

das Geschäft   die Geschäft**e**   der Einkauf   die Eink**ä**ufe

However there are many irregular plurals in German, and these are best learned as you come across them.

Agreement of adjectives

If an adjective comes before a noun rather than after it, then the adjective takes the ending **-e** before a singular noun and **-en** before a plural noun:

Die Schokolade ist heiß.	Die heiß**e** Schokolade.	The hot chocolate.
Der Rock is blau.	Der blau**e** Rock.	The blue skirt.
Das Kleid ist neu.	Das neu**e** Kleid.	The new dress.
Die Geschäfte sind schön.	Die schön**en** Geschäfte.	The nice store.

But note that without an article (i.e., "the"), you say:
Schön**e** Geschäfte, dropping the **-n**.

The direct object pronoun

When a masculine word is the object of a sentence, then the word for "the" or "a," etc., takes an **-n** in German:

Der Rock ist Blau.	Ich nehme de**n** Rock.	I'll take the skirt.
	Ich suche eine**n** Rock.	I'm looking for a skirt.
Mein Bruder heißt Thomas.	Wir treffen meine**n** Bruder.	We're meeting my brother.

This, these

The word for "this" in German is **dieser**. It changes in much the same way as **der**.

dieser Käse (m)	this cheese	**diese** Butter (f)	this butter
dieses Ei (n)	this egg	**diese** Kekse (pl)	these cookies

Verbs with a vowel change

Some German verbs have a change of vowel in the part which goes with **er/sie/es**:

treffen (to meet): er tr**i**fft   tragen (to wear, carry): sie tr**ä**gt
helfen (to help): er h**i**lft   schlafen (to sleep): sie schl**ä**ft

things to do

2.1 You are with a group of tourists at a German hotel, and the only person who speaks the language. The waiter asks "Was möchten Sie?" Order breakfast for everyone else. The first one is done for you.

1 Deidre: a boiled egg, rolls with butter and jam, a pot of coffee.
   Ein gekochtes Ei, Brötchen mit Butter und Marmelade, ein
   Kännchen Kaffee.
2 Jeremy: bacon and eggs, toast and honey, black coffee.
4 Laura: rye bread, ham, tea with lemon.
5 John: orange juice, a piece of toast with orange marmalade, a
   cup of tea with milk.
6 Chantal: bread, cheese and hot chocolate.

2.2 You are out shopping to buy food for a picnic and manage to find
everything you want at the same shop. Can you tell how much money
you'll need?

> **Preise**
> Eier: 1,50/Packung
> Milch: 1,00/Liter
> Käse: 8,40/Kilo
> Mehl: 1,90/Paket
> Speiseöl: 1,80/Flasche
> Schokolade: 1,20/Tafel
> Äpfel: 2,60/Kilo

2.3 Gisela is shopping for new clothes, but nothing that Helen suggests
seems to be right. Imagine you are Gisela. What would you say in
German?
1 Helen: Die gelbe Bluse ist sehr modisch (fashionable).
   Gisela: [But it's too tight.]
2 Helen: Ich habe die blauen Jeans gern.
   Gisela: [They're too expensive.]
3 Helen: Hast du den grauen Regenmantel gern?
   Gisela   [Doesn't like the color.]
4 Helen   Das rosa Sweatshirt paßt dir (fits you) ausgeziechnet.
   Gisela: [She'll take it.]

ORDERING A MEAL

Eating   Lunch is generally the main meal in German homes, supper being a cold meal similar to breakfast. In restaurants, dinner is served from about 6 to 9:30 p.m. (later in larger ones). Look out for the **Menü** (full dinner) which usually consists of 3 courses, often starting with a filling soup. Main courses may consist of potatoes cooked in a variety of different ways, vegetables and meat. Pork is popular in Germany, lamb is less so and shellfish are not common. There are hundreds of varieties of sausage (**Wurst**), as well as smoked meats and pickled fish. Most cities have many ethnic restaurants, such as Chinese, Greek and Italian.

Restaurant bills normally include tax and a 10% tip (**Bedienung Inbegriffen**), but is is normal to round up the amount, or leave a small tip.

im Restaurant/at the restaurant

George Jackson has a free evening after the opening of the Sports Convention. Ulrike and Ludwig Bauer have invited him to eat at a restaurant.

Ulrike:	**Hier ist ein Tisch für drei Personen**, am Fenster.
Kellnerin:	(approaching) Bitte schön, meine Damen und Herren?
Ulrike:	**Die Speisekarte, bitte, und die Weinkarte.**

Kellnerin:	Gerne. (Handing the menu) Ich empfehle Ihnen die Frikadellen, unsere Spezialität. Sie schmecken sehr gut.
Ludwig:	Einen Moment, bitte. **Gibt es ein Tagesgedeck?**
Kellnerin:	Nein, nicht am Abend.

(Filetsteak mit Pommes Frites)

SPEISEKARTE

VORSPEISEN	Russische Eier	deviled eggs
	Wurstplatte	assorted cold cuts
SUPPEN	Hühnerbrühe	chicken broth
	Nudelsuppe	noodle soup
FLEISCHSPEISEN	Kalbsbraten mit Salzkartoffeln	roast veal with boiled potatoes
	Frikadellen mit Butterreis	meatballs with buttered rice
	und gemischtem Salat/	and mixed salad/
	oder Gemüse	or vegetables
	Filetsteak mit pommes Frites	steak and French fries
FISCHGERICHTE	Gebackene Forelle mit Pilzen	baked trout with mushrooms
	Panierte Scholle mit	breaded flounder with
	Petersilienkartoffeln	parsley potatoes
NACHTISCH	Käsekuchen	cheesecake
	Obsttorte	fruit torte
	Schokoladeneis	chocolate ice cream

Kellnerin:	Möchten Sie bestellen?
Ludwig:	Hmm, Ulrike. Was nimmst du?
Ulrike:	**Ich möchte** Nudelsuppe, **und dann** Frikadellen.
Ludwig:	**Ich mag keine Suppe.** Russische Eier und Kalbsbraten **für mich.** Na George, was essen Sie gern—Fleisch oder Fisch?
George:	**Ich hätte gern** Filetsteak mit Pommes Frites. Keine Vorspeise für mich!
Kellnerin:	Also, gut. Und zum trinken, meine Damen und Herren?
Ulrike:	**Bringen Sie uns bitte eine Flasche Weißwein,**—Rheinwein.
George:	Entschuldigen Sie, ich trinke nicht so gern Wein. Ich trinke lieber ein Glas Bier.
Ludwig:	Ich auch—**zweimal Bier,** bitte, und **ein Glas Wein** für meine Frau.
Ulrike:	(To George) Essen Sie gern Torte, George? Die Obsttorte ist hier ausgezeichnet.
George:	Oh ja! Aber **ich esse lieber** Käsekuchen.
Ludwig:	Wie Thomas. Er nimmt immer Käsekuchen.
Ulrike:	Mit Schlagsahne!

Getting a table

Haben Sie einen Tisch für drei Personen?	Do you have a table for three?
am Fenster/auf der Terrasse/in der Ecke	by the window/on the terrace/in the corner
Ich möchte einen Tisch reservieren.	I'd like to reserve a table.

Ordering

Bitte schön, meine Damen und Herren?	What would you like (ladies and gentlemen)?
Die Speisekarte und die Weinkarte	The menu and the wine list
Gibt es ein Tagesgedeck?	Is there a special today?
ein Touristen-Menü?	a tourist menu?
Ich empfehle Ihnen . . .	I recommend . . .
Sie schmecken sehr gut.	They taste very good.
Möchten Sie bestellen?	Would you like to order?
Was nimmst du?	What will you have?
Was essen Sie gern—Fleisch oder Fisch?	What would you like, meat or fish?
Was für Gemüse gibt es?	What kinds of vegetables are there?
Gibt es vegetarische Gerichte?	Are there any vegetarian dishes?
Ich nehme eine Portion Bohnen.	I'll have an order of beans.
Ich hätte gern/ich möchte/ich esse gern . . .	I'd like . . .
Ich mag/ich mag kein/e/en . . .	I like/don't like . . .
Keine Vorspeise für mich.	No appetizer for me.
Einmal das Gedeck.	One today's special.

Ordering drinks

Und zum trinken?	And to drink?
Bringen Sie uns eine Flasche Weißwein/Rheinwein.	Bring us a bottle of white wine/Rhine wine.
Ich trinke nicht so gern Wein.	I'm not very fond of wine.
Ich trinke lieber ein Glas Bier.	I'd rather have a glass of beer.
Zweimal Bier.	Two beers.

Desserts

Dreimal Schokoladeneis.	Three chocolate ice creams.
Die Obsttorte ist ausgezeichnet.	The fruit torte is excellent.
Ich esse lieber Käsekuchen.	I prefer cheesecake.
Mit Schlagsahne	With whipped cream
Wo sind die Toiletten, bitte?	Where are the toilets?
Fräulein/Herr Ober!	Waiter/waitress!
Die Rechnung, bitte.	The bill, please.
Ist Bedienung inbegriffen?	Is the tip included?
Extraaufschlag	extra (charge)
Mehrwertsteuer	tax
das Trinkgeld	tip
Guten Appetit!	Bon appétit!

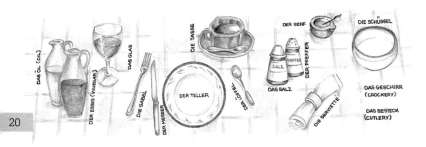

FOOD, DRINK AND SNACKS

Understanding the menu

(Different types of food are listed on page 79.)
The words for German dishes are often a mixture of several terms. In order to understand a menu, it is useful to know a few cooking expressions:

gebacken	baked	gegrillt	grilled
geräuchert	smoked	gekocht	boiled
gedämpft	steamed	gefüllt	stuffed
gebraten	fried/roasted	überbacken	au gratin

Die Würste (sausages)

die Weißwurst	veal sausage	die Frankfurter	frankfurter
die Zungenwurst	tongue sausage	die Wienerli	Viennese frankfurter

Die Nachtisch (dessert)

das Eis	ice cream
das Vanillen/Zitronen/ Schokoladeneis	vanilla/lemon/ chocolate ice cream
der Apfelstrudel	apple strudel
Schwarzwälder Kirschtorte	Black Forest cake
der Obstsalat	fruit salad
das Kompott	fruit compote
Gugelhupf	raisin and almond cake
die Sachertorte	chocolate cake
der Eisbecher	ice cream sundae
Pfirsich Melba	peach melba
Pfannkuchen	pancakes
Apfelkuchen	apple cake
die Torte/der Kuchen	pie/cake

There are many national and regional specialities in Germany, Austria and Switzerland.

Die Getränke (drinks)

ein Glas Bier (n)	a glass of beer	eine Flasche Sekt	a bottle of sparkling wine
ein Bier vom Faß	draft beer		
ein helles Bier	Weiss beer	ein Kognak (m)	brandy
ein dunkles Bier	dark beer	ein Likör (m)	liqueur
ein Altbier	bitter ale	ein Glühwein (m)	mulled wine
ein Pilsener	lager	ein Wodka (m)	vodka
ein Glas Wein (m)	a glass of wine	ein Whisky (m)	whisky
eine Karaffe Wein	a carafe of wine	ein Portwein (m)	port
der Rotwein	red wine	ein Apfelwein (m)	cider
der Weißwein	white wine	ein Kirschwasser (n)	cherry brandy
der Rosé	rosé	ein Schnaps (m)	schnapps
trocken/süß	dry/sweet	ein Glas Wasser (n)	a glass of water

Cafés and snacks Coffee and cake (*Kaffee und Kuchen*) is served between 3 and 5 p.m. in a **Café (Kaffeehaus** in Austria) or tea room attached to a **Konditorei**. There are many varieties of delicious cakes, often filled with cream and liqueurs, to choose from. Cafés and bars are open all day, and sell alcoholic as well as nonalcoholic drinks, tea, coffee, etc. Cafés normally have waiter service, and price lists of drinks are displayed in the window. Look out for the **Bierstube** (similar to a pub) and **Weinstube** (wine bar). For snacks, go to an **Imbißstube** (snack bar) or **Bratwurststand** (sausage stand), where you can get rolls filled with sausage and other fillings, as well as potato salad and soft drinks.

Ich habe Hunger; ich habe Durst (I'm hungry/thirsty)

Of course, you might not want to order a full meal. Here are some common snacks.

ein Sandwich (m)	sandwich	eine Zervelat-wurst	smoked sausage
ein Schinkenbrot (n)	ham sandwich	ein (deutsches) Beefsteak (n)	hamburger
ein Käsebrötchen (n)	a roll with cheese	ein Halbes Hähnchen	½ chicken
ein Omelett (n) mit Schinken/ Käse/Pilzen	ham/cheese/ mushroom omelet	Matjeshering (m)	salt herring
		Heringsalat (m)	herring salad
Käseschnitte (f)	cheese on toast	Kartoffelsalat	potato salad
Kartoffelchips	potato chips	Strammer Max	smoked ham and fried eggs on bread
Pommes Frites	french fries		
eine Pizza	pizza		
eine Bratwurst	pork sausage	ein Schaschlik (m)	shish kebab
eine Frankfurter	frankfurter	DURCHGEH-ENDER DIENST	24-hour service
eine Bockwurst	large frankfurter		
eine Currywurst	curried sausage		

Kalte Getränke (cold drinks)

eine Flasche . . .	a bottle of
ein Glas	a glass of
zwei Glas	two glasses of
eine Tasse . . .	a cup of
vier Tasse . . .	four cups of
eine Limonade	soda
eine Cola	cola
ein Mineralwasser (n)	mineral water
ein Orangen-sprudel (m)	orange soda
ein Fruchtsaft	fruit juice
ein Apfelsaft	apple juice
ein Traubensaft	grape juice
ein Tomatensaft	tomato juice
ein Eistee	iced tea
ein Glas Milch	glass of milk
ein Bananenshake	banana milkshake
ein Ananasshake	pineapple shake

the way it works

Es gibt

The expression es gibt means ''there is''/''there are'' and is followed by a noun as object. Gibt es ein**en** Tisch am Fenster?   Is there a table by the window?

Kein

If you want to say you don't have something, or you don't want something, and so on, then you use **kein**. It works the same way as **ein**:

Eine Vorspeise für Ludwig.	An appetizer for Ludwig.
Keine Vorspeise für George.	No appetizer for George.
Wir haben ein Tagesgedeck.	We have a special of the day.
Wir haben **kein** Tagesgedeck.	We don't have a special of the day.
Haben Sie einen Tisch frei?	Do you have a table free?
Wir haben **keinen** Tisch frei.	We don't have a table free.
Gibt es heute Birnen?	Are there any pears today?
Nein, es gibt **keine** Birnen.	No, there aren't any pears.

Pronouns as objects

''Me'' and ''him'' are objects of the sentence:
I see him   Ich sehe **ihn**
He sees me   Er sieht **mich**
In German, pronouns take the object (or accusative) case after the preposition **für**. Use these expressions in German to say ''for me,'' ''for him,'' etc.

für mich	for me	**für uns**	for us
für Sie	for you	**für Sie**	for you (pl)
für dich	for you (fam.)		
für ihn/sie/es	for him/her/it	**für sie**	for them

Some more verbs

Here are some more common verbs you have seen in this unit.

nehmen *to take*

ich **nehme**	I take	wir **nehmen**	we take
Sie **nehmen**	you take	Sie **nehmen**	you take (pl)
du **nimmst**	you take (fam.)		
er/sie/es **nimmt**	he/she/it takes	sie **nehmen**	they take

geben *to give*

ich **gebe**	I give	wir **geben**	we give
Sie **geben**	you give	Sie **geben**	you give
du **gibst**	you give		
er/sie/es **gibt**	he/she/it gives	sie **geben**	they give

essen *to eat*

ich **esse**	I eat	wir **essen**	we eat
Sie **essen**	you eat	Sie **essen**	you eat
du **ißt**	you eat		
er/sie/es **ißt**	he/she/it eats	sie **essen**	they eat

Some German verbs add an **e** before the final **t** in the part which goes with **er/sie/es**: arbeiten (to work)—er arbeit**et**; finden (to find)—sie find**et**; kosten (to cost)—es kost**et**; senden (to send)—er send**et**.

The imperative

If you are telling someone to do something or giving someone an order, then you are using the imperative. In German, this is very easy:

Bringen Sie mir ein Glas Bier! Bring me a glass of beer!
Nehmen Sie das Gepäck! Take the luggage!
Vergessen Sie nicht meine Einkäufe! Don't forget my shopping!
Gisela, **vergiß nicht** meine Einkäufe! Gisela, don't forget my shopping!

things to do

2.4 Ich habe keinen Hunger

A colleague, Dieter, wants to go out to a restaurant, but you are not feeling very hungry. See if you can put your preferences into German:

1 Dieter: Ich esse gern ein Filetsteak mit Kartoffeln und gemischtem Salat. Und Sie?
[Say you'd rather have a ham sandwich and potato chips.]

2 Dieter: Ich esse gern gebackene Seezunge mit Pellkartoffeln und Pilzen. Und Sie?
[Tell him you'd prefer a cheese omelette and french fries.]

3 Dieter: Ich hätte gern Eisbein, Knödel und Karotten. Sie nicht?
[Say you'd rather eat a hamburger and potato salad.]

4 Dieter: Ich esse gern ein Wiener Schnitzel mit Pommes Frites und Erbsen, und dann einen großen Eisbecher! Sie auch?
[Say no, you'd rather have a sausage with curry sauce.]

2.5 Und zum trinken?

You are ordering drinks at a café for a group of German friends. Point to each in turn, saying what he or she would like, e.g.:

Ingrid: **für sie, ein Glas Traubensaft**

1 Heinz: 5 Gudrun:

2 Christa: 6 Klaus:

3 Kerstin and Norbert: 7 Hartmut and Bernd:

4 Jürgen

ASKING FOR AND GIVING DIRECTIONS

City Transportation   There are subway systems (**die U-Bahn**) in ten German cities, and some have street car networks (**die S-Bahn**). Tickets for both are normally bought from vending machines and may have to be punched to validate (**FAHRKARTEN ENTWERTEN**) before boarding. Street car tickets can be purchased at their stops. You may be able to buy a **Mehrfahrkarte** (a ticket valid for up to five trips) or a daily pass for unlimited travel, and the same tickets can normally be used on subways, street cars and buses for trips in one direction.

fahren mit der U-Bahn/taking the subway

George Jackson is setting out early in the morning to the trade fair. He asks a passerby for directions.

George: Entschuldigen Sie bitte. Ich besuche das Messegelände. **Wie komme ich am besten zu** . . . uh . . . (looks at his instructions) der Theresienhöhe?

Passant: Wie, bitte? Die Theresienhöhe? (Thinks) Von hier fahren Sie am besten mit der U-Bahn. Die nächste Station ist Marienplatz.

George: **Wo ist das?**

Passant: Gehen Sie hier die Straße entlang, und dann links in die Residenzstraße—das ist die dritte Straße links, glaube ich. Die U-Bahnstation ist ungefähr nach zweihundert Metern, auf der rechten Seite.

George: (looking bemused) Auf der rechten Seite?
Passant: Ah, Sie haben einen Stadtplan. Zeigen Sie mir—wir sind hier, Maximilianstraße; hier ist der Marienplatz, und hier ist die U-Bahnstation Messegelände.
George: Ja, ich verstehe. Sagen Sie mir, **muß ich umsteigen**?
Passant: Ja. Sie müssen im Hauptbahnhof umsteigen, und dann haben Sie nur zwei Stationen. Sie sind bald dort.
George: Und wie komme ich in die Ausstellung?
Passant: Die Ausstellungshalle ist genau gegenüber.
George: Vielen Dank.
Passant: Bitte Schön.

How do I get there?

Wie komme ich am besten . . .	What's the best way to get . . .
in die Mozartstraße	to Mozartstraße
nach Stuttgart	to Stuttgart
zum Bahnhof	to the train station
zum Flughafen	to the airport
zur Theresienhöhe	to Theresienhöhe
zur Universität?	to the university?

Asking for and understanding instructions

Ist das der richtige Weg zum Hafen?	Is that the right way to the harbor?
Ich suche den Dom	I'm looking for the cathedral
Wo ist . . . ?	Where is . . . ?
Wo finde ich . . . ?	Where do I find . . . ?
Wie weit ist das?	How far is that?
Es ist ungefähr noch zweihundert Meter.	It's about 200 meters (ahead).
Es ist nach zweihundert Metern auf der rechten Seite.	It's 200 meters ahead on the right-hand side.
Sie müssen zurück.	You must go back.
Es ist nah/weit.	It's near/far.
Gehen Sie hier die Straße entlang.	Go down the street.
Gehen Sie geradeaus.	Go straight ahead.
Dann links/rechts in die Residenzstraße	Then left/right onto Residenzstraße
Gehen Sie wieder rechts.	Go right again.
Nehmen Sie die zweite Straße links/die dritte Straße rechts.	Take the second street on the left/third on the right
gleich rechts/links	immediately on the right/left

da drüben/gegenüber	over there/opposite
bei der Kreuzung/Ampel	at the intersection/lights
um die Ecke	at the corner
hinter dem Postamt	behind the post office
neben der Kirche	near the church
nicht weit von . . . entfernt	not far from . . .
Die Polizeiwache liegt auf der linken Seite.	The police station is on the left.

Using a map

Sie haben einen Stadtplan.	You have a map.
Wir sind hier, und hier ist . . .	We're here, and here is . . .
Sie sind bald dort.	You'll soon be there.
Sie sind in zehn Minuten dort.	You'll be there in 10 minutes.
Die Ausstellungshalle ist genau gegenüber.	The exhibition hall is right across.
zu Fuß gehen	to walk
Ich will zum Zoo gehen.	I want to go to the zoo.
Zum Zoo ist es zu weit.	It's too far to the zoo.
Wir können zu Fuß in den Park gehen	We can walk to the park.
der Fußgänger/die Fußgängerzone	pedestrian/pedestrian zone

Traveling on public transportation

Von hier fahren Sie am besten.	From here it's best to go . . .
mit der U-Bahn/S-Bahn/	by subway/street car
mit dem Bus	by bus
mit dem Zug/mit dem Auto	by train/by car
(fliegen Sie) mit dem Flugzeug	by plane

On the subway

Wo ist die nächste U-Bahnstation?	Where is the nearest subway station?
Die nächste Station ist Marienplatz.	The next station is Marienplatz.
Können Sie mir zeigen?	Can you show me?
Muß ich umsteigen?	Do I have to transfer?
Sie müssen im Hauptbahnhof umsteigen.	You have to change at the main train station.
Sie haben Umsteigemöglichkeiten . . .	There are connections . . .
in Richtung	in the direction of
Dann haben Sie nur zwei Stationen	Then you've got only 2 stations
einsteigen/aussteigen.	to get on/off.

USEFUL WORDS AND EXPRESSIONS

Ich besuche das Messegelände.	I'm visiting the convention center.
die Messe	convention
Zeigen Sie mir.	Show me.
Ja, ich verstehe	Yes, I understand.
Sagen Sie mir	Tell me
die Ausstellung	the exhibition

the way it works

Some more verbs

müssen *to have to, must*		**können** *to be able to, can*	
ich **muß** *I must*	wir **müssen**	ich **kann** *I can*	wir **können**
du **mußt**	Sie **müssen** (pl.)	du **kannst**	Sie **können**
Sie **müssen**		Sie **können**	
er/sie/es **muß**	sie **müssen**	er/sie/es **kann**	sie **können**

fahren *to go, drive*			
ich **fahre**	I go	wir **fahren**	we go
du **fährst**	you go	Sie **fahren**	you go (pl.)
Sie **fahren**	you go		
er/sie/es **fährt**	he/she/it goes	sie **fahren**	they go

Word order

You will have noticed in the dialogue that the order of words is not always the same as in English.

1 In German, the verb must always be the ˙second idea in any sentence. Therefore, if something other than the subject comes first, the verb is turned around so that it will still be in second place:
Sie fahren mit der U-Bahn *but* Von hier **fahren Sie** mit der U-Bahn.

2 When a sentence contains a verb followed by a second verb in the infinitive, then the infinitive goes to the end:
Sie **müssen** im Hauptbahnhof **umsteigen**. You have to change at the main train station.

Verbs of motion

If you are talking about going to or from somewhere, then you will be using a verb of motion. **In** after a verb of motion is followed by **der/die/das** in the object case. (Note that you use **gehen** when going somewhere on foot, and **fahren** when using some kind of transportation.

Ich gehe in den Park (m.)   I'm going into the park.

Mit, zu, in

You will have seen how **der/die/das** change after such words as **mit** (with), **zu** (to, towards) and **in** (in, at, into). This is how it works:

der Zug (m)	**mit dem** Zug
das Taxi (n)	**mit dem** Taxi
die U-Bahn (f)	**mit der** U-Bahn

der Taxistand (m)	**zum** (zu + dem) Taxistand
das Kino (n)	**zum** (zu + dem) Kino
die Haltestelle (f)	**zur** (zu + der) Haltestelle

der Bahnhof (m)	**im** (in + dem) Bahnhof	in the train station
das Museum (n)	**im** (in + dem) Museum	in the museum
die Kirche (f)	**in der** Kirche	in the church

However, if you are going *into* the train station, museum or church, then you would be using a verb of motion, and **in** would be followed by the object case.

things to do

3.1 Here are the names of some places you will find useful when asking for or giving someone else directions:

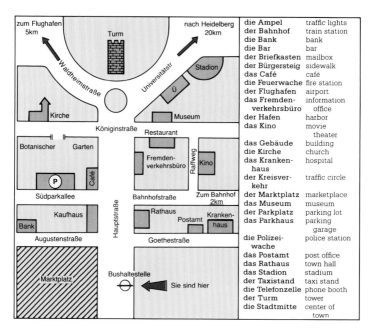

die Ampel	traffic lights
der Bahnhof	train station
die Bank	bank
die Bar	bar
der Briefkasten	mailbox
der Bürgersteig	sidewalk
das Café	café
die Feuerwache	fire station
der Flughafen	airport
das Fremden- verkehrsbüro	information office
der Hafen	harbor
das Kino	movie theater
das Gebäude	building
die Kirche	church
das Kranken- haus	hospital
der Kreisver- kehr	traffic circle
der Marktplatz	marketplace
das Museum	museum
der Parkplatz	parking lot
das Parkhaus	parking garage
die Polizei- wache	police station
das Postamt	post office
das Rathaus	town hall
das Stadion	stadium
der Taxistand	taxi stand
die Telefonzelle	phone booth
der Turm	tower
die Stadtmitte	center of town

You are at the bus stop on the map and overhear a German lady giving these directions to three passersby. Look at the map. Can you tell where they want to go?

1 Gehen Sie hier die Straße entlang, dann rechts in die Königinstraße, und Sie sehen es gleich links.

2 Sie gehen geradeaus, dann die erste Straße links. Er liegt auf den rechten Seite, um die Ecke.

3 Nehmen Sie die erste Straße rechts, und es ist links, neben dem Postamt.

3.2 A number of German visitors at your hotel in Goethestraße are puzzling over the best way of getting to various places. How would you advise them? The first one is done for you.

1 Wie komme ich am besten zum Bahnhof?   Sie fahren am besten mit dem Bus.

2 ... in die Königinstraße?   5 ... zur Universität?
3 ... zum Flughafen?   6 ... zum Krankenhaus?
4 ... nach Heidelberg?

nachmittags/in the afternoon

TRAVELING BY BUS

▶ ▶ ▶ **Bus and taxi**   Buses tend to be local only, and tickets can be bought
when boarding, or from vending machines. However, there are a few
long-distance bus companies, mainly on tourist or scenic routes (e.g.,
Deutsche Touring).

All taxis have meters. You can get a taxi from a stand (**Taxistand**) or by
telephoning a **Taxizentrale**. It is typical to tip taxi drivers, and in large
cities, drivers are accustomed to giving foreign business travelers a
receipt (**eine Quittung**) from which sales tax can be reclaimed.

ein Tag in München/a day in Munich

Ulrike Bauer has been showing Helen some of the sights of Munich,
together with Gisela and Karl-Heinrich.

Ulrike:	Es gibt hier in München noch viel zu sehen, Helen—das Deutsche Museum, das Bayerische Museum, die Frauenkirche, die Heiliggeistkirche . . .
Gisela:	(groaning) In London hat man auch Museen und Kirchen, Mutti!
Ulrike:	(looking at her watch) **Es ist schon ein Uhr**—essen wir unser Picknick . . . Wir haben auch herrliche Parks, Helen. Der Englische Garten is sehr schön, und der Olympiapark ist interessant.

Karl-Heinrich:	Ich will zum Zoo gehen.
Ulrike:	Nein, Liebchen, zum Zoo ist es zu weit. Aber wir können zu Fuß in den Park gehen.
Gisela:	Wir sind so müde. Hier ist eine Bushaltestelle, da drüben: nehmen wir den Bus. **Welcher Bus fährt zur Universität**, Mutti?
Ulrike:	Wir brauchen die Linie achtzehn. Aha, hier kommt unser Bus. Schnell, meine Kinder!

The time

Wieviel Uhr ist es?	What time is it?
Wie spät ist es?	What time is it?
Es ist zwei Uhr.	It's two o'clock.
Es ist fünf Minuten nach zwei.	It's five minutes after two.
Es ist viertel nach zwei.	It's a quarter after two.
Es ist zwanzig nach zwei.	It's twenty past two.
Es ist fünf vor halb drei.	It's twenty-five past two.
Es ist halb drei.	It's half past two.
Es ist fünf nach halb drei.	It's twenty-five to three.
Es ist viertel vor drei.	It's a quarter to three.
Es ist zehn vor drei.	It's ten to three.
Es ist drei Uhr.	It's three o'clock.
vormittags/nachmittags	in the morning/afternoon
abends/nachts	in the evening/at night
Es ist Mittag/Mitternacht.	It's noon/midnight

Note that in German, **halb drei** (half three) is used for "half past two." "Half past three" would be **halb vier**, and so on; **halb eins** = half past twelve; **ein Uhr** = one o'clock.

The twenty-four clock is used when referring to train schedules, etc.:

Um wieviel Uhr fährt der Zug ab?	What time does the train leave?
Um wieviel Uhr kommt der Bus an?	What time does the bus arrive?
Um vierzehn Uhr zehn.	At 14:10.
Der Zug fährt um siebzehn Uhr fünfunddreissig.	The train leaves at 17:35.

Useful expressions of time

vorgestern	the day before yesterday
vor drei Tagen	3 days ago
gestern/heute/morgen	yesterday/today/tomorrow
übermorgen	the day after tomorrow
heute morgen	this morning
heute nachmittag	this afternoon
heute abend	this evening
morgen früh	tomorrow morning
jeden Tag/jede Woche	every day/every week

31

Taking a bus

Nehmen wir den Bus.	Let's take the bus.
Hier ist eine Bushaltestelle.	Here's a bus stop.
Gibt es eine Bushaltestelle in der Nähe?	Is there a bus stop nearby?
Wann gehen die Busse nach . . . ?	When do the buses go to . . . ?
Welcher Bus fährt nach Bremen/zur Universität?	Which bus goes to Bremen/to the University?
Fährt dieser Bus nach Koblenz?	Is this bus going to Koblenz?
Sie brauchen die Linie sechsunddreißig.	You need a number 36 bus.
Wo muß ich aussteigen?	Where do I get off?
Bitte aussteigen!	Everybody off, please.

USEFUL WORDS AND EXPRESSIONS

Es gibt noch viel zu sehen.	There's still a lot more to see.
das Deutsche Museum/das Bayerische Museum	the German Museum/the Bavarian Museum
die Frauenkirche/die Heiliggeistkirche	the Church of Our Lady/the Church of the Holy Ghost
In Boston hat man auch Museen und Kirchen.	They have museums and churches in Boston, too.
Es ist schon ein Uhr.	It's one o'clock already.
Essen wir unser Picknick.	Let's eat our picnic.
Der Englische Garten ist sehr schön.	The English Garden is splendid.
Der Olympiapark ist interessant.	The Olympic Park is interesting.
Ich will zum Zoo gehen.	I want to go to the zoo.
Liebchen/Liebling	darling
Wir sind so müde.	We're so tired.
Schnell, meine Kinder	Quick, children

TRAVELING BY TRAIN

in der Schalterhalle/at the ticket office

Günther, a friend from Stuttgart, is coming to visit Thomas Bauer in Munich. He buys a train ticket.

Schalterbeamtin:	Bitte schön?
Günther:	Guten Tag! **Eine Fahrkarte nach München**, bitte.
Schalterbeamtin:	Einmal nach München . . . einfach, oder hin und zurück?
Günther:	**Hin and zurück. Was macht das**, bitte?
Schalterbeamtin:	Zweite Klasse . . . das macht sechzig Mark und fünfzig Pfennig.
Günther:	**Wann fährt der nächste Zug** nach München?
Schalterbeamtin:	Der nächste Zug fährt um vierzehn Uhr zehn.

Günther:	**Von welchem Gleis?**
Schalterbeamtin:	Das weiß ich nicht. Normalerweise von Gleis drei oder vier. Sie müssen das Anschlagbrett lesen.
Günther:	**Muß ich umsteigen?**
Schalterbeamtin:	Nein, nein . . . (shaking her head) Was für ein ängstlicher junger Mann!
Günther:	(reading the notice board) **D-Zug nach München**, vierzehn Uhr zehn, Abfahrt Gleis fünf. (looking at his watch) Es ist nun fünf Minuten nach zwei—ich habe keine Zeit . . .
Schalterbeamtin:	Doch, Sie haben gerade noch Zeit!

Traveling by train

die Schalterbeamtin	ticket agent (female)
Eine Fahrkarte/ein Fahrschein nach München, bitte.	A ticket to Munich, please.
Einfach, oder hin und zurück?	One-way or round-trip?
eine Einzelfahrkarte	a one-way ticket
eine Rückfahrkarte	a round-trip ticket
erste Klasse/zweite Klasse	first/second class
Was macht das?	What does that come to?
Wann fährt der nächste Zug nach München?	When is the next train to Munich?
Der nächste Zug fährt um vierzehn Uhr.	The next train is at 14:00.
Kann ich einen Sitzplatz reservieren?	Can I reserve a seat?
Von welchem Gleis?	From which track?
Normalerweise von Gleis drei.	Usually from track 3.
Sie müssen das Anschlagbrett lesen.	You'll have to check the notice board.
D-Zug nach München, Abfahrt Gleis fünf.	Express train to Munich, departure from track 5.
Muß ich umsteigen?	Do I have to change trains?

33

Das weiß ich nicht.	I don't know.
Was für ein ängstlicher junger Mann.	What an anxious young man.
Ich habe keine Zeit.	I don't have time
Doch, Sie haben gerade noch Zeit!	Yes, you've just got time!

Train travel   Not surprisingly, the train systems of Germany, Austria, and Switzerland are all generally fast, clean, comfortable, and very punctual. These trains have the added bonus of offering views of often breathtaking scenery.

If you're planning extensive travel, there are several railpass options available for a wide variety of itineraries and budgets. Passes such as the GermanRail Pass or the Austrian Railpass offer other benefits such as discounted fares on buses, steamer ships, and bike rentals.

In Germany, the modern train system is run by Deutsche Bahn. Almost all of the trains have telephone service and a snack bar or dining car, which serves beer, wine, and both German and international cuisine. Many of the seats recline for comfort on long journeys. Both smoking (**raucher**) and nonsmoking (**nichtraucher**) compartments are available.

Deutsche Bahn runs several high-speed trains that can make for a quicker journey than flying on an airplane. If you are planning to travel on one of these trains, it's important to make a reservation whenever possible, especially for any overnight trains.

ICE	Inter City Express	The fastest and most modern in the German train system. These trains travel at speeds of up to 280 km/hr (174 miles/hr).
IC	Inter City	Offers express service between large- and medium-sized German cities.
EC	Euro City	Connects Germany with 13 other European countries.

Watch for these notices:

ABFAHRT	departures	**BESETZT**	occupied
ANKUNFT	arrivals	**FAHRKARTEN**	tickets
AUSKUNFT ·	information	**FAHRKARTEN-**	ticket machine
GLEIS 3	track 3	**AUTOMAT**	
BAHNSTEIG 9	platform 9	**RAUCHER**	smoker
FREI	vacant	**NICHTRAUCHER**	nonsmoker

the way it works

Verbs

vergessen *to forget*	
ich **vergesse** *I forget* wir **vergessen**	
du **vergißt** Sie **vergessen**	
Sie **vergessen**	
er/sie/es **vergißt** sie **vergessen**	

sehen *to see*	
ich **sehe** *I see*	wir **sehen**
du **siehst**	Sie **sehen**
Sie **sehen**	
er/sie/es **sieht**	sie **sehen**

Man

In German, **man** means "one," "people," "you," "they," etc.:

In Denver hat **man** auch Museen.	They have museums in Denver too.
Man kann zu Fuß in den Park gehen.	You can walk to the park.
Man kann das nicht sagen.	One can't say that.

Adjectives

When following **ein, mein** etc., adjectives take these endings:

masc.	*fem.*	*neuter*
ein herrlich**er** Park	eine alt**e** Kirche	ein interessant**es** Museum
mein jung**er** Mann	meine klein**e** Schwester	mein lieb**es** Kind

Welcher (which)

Welcher works like **dieser**:

welcher Zug (m)	which train	**welche** Straße (f)	which street
welches Boot (n)	which boat	**welche** Busse (pl.)	which buses

things to do

3.3 You want to go to Frankfurt. Ask the ticket agent:
1 When is the next train to Frankfurt?
2 From which track?
3 Do you have to change trains?
   What time does it arrive? (**ankommen**)
5 Can you reserve a seat?

CHANGING MONEY

▶▶▶ **Currency exchange** In Germany, banking hours are 8:30 a.m.–1:00 p.m. and 2:30 p.m.–4:00 p.m. from Monday to Friday (5:30 on Thursdays). Currency exchanges (**Wechselstube**) at borders, train stations, and airports are generally open longer but will not offer the best exchange rate.

ATMs are a convenient way to withdraw money while traveling throughout Germany, Austria, and Switzerland. Credit cards are widely accepted in shops, hotels, and restaurants.

The German unit of currency, the Deutsche Mark (DM) is divided into 100 Pfennige.

in der Bank/at the bank

Helen wants to buy some stamps for her postcards, but first Ulrike takes her to the bank to change some money.

Bankbeamter:	Guten Morgen. Was wünschen Sie, bitte?
Helen:	Guten Morgen. **Ich möchte einen Reisescheck einlösen**.
Bankbeamter:	Sehr gut. Ihren Paß, bitte.
Helen:	Sie brauchen meinen Paß? Er ist zu Hause!

Bankbeamter:	Es tut mir leid, aber ohne einen Paß konnen wir Reiseschecks nicht einlösen.
Helen:	Dann möchte ich **zwanzig Pfund in Deutsche Mark wechseln.**
Bankbeamter:	Wollen Sie bitte dieses Formular ausfüllen, und unterschreiben Sie hier. (While Helen is writing) So, Sie sind Engländerin.
Helen:	Ja, aus London. Bitte, **wie ist der Wechselkurs heute?**
Bankbeamter:	Er steht auf dem Anschlagbrett da drüben. Nehmen Sie dieses Papier und gehen Sie zur Kasse —dort wird man Ihnen das Geld geben.

Geldwechseln (changing money)

die Bank/die Sparkasse	the bank/savings bank
der Bankbeamte	bank teller
Ich möchte einen Reisescheck einlösen.	I'd like to cash a Traveler's check.
Kann ich meine Scheck einlösen?	Can I cash my check?
Ich möchte zwanzig Dollar in Deutsche Mark (um)wechseln/eintauschen.	I'd like to change $20 into Marks.
Wollen Sie bitte dieses Formular ausfüllen?	Fill out this form please.
Unterschreiben Sie hier.	Sign here.

Exchange rates

Wie ist der Wechselkurs?	What is the exchange rate?
Er steht auf dem Anschlagbrett.	It's on the notice board.
Was macht das?	What does it come to?
Fünfundzwanzig Mark achtzig Pfennig	25 Marks and 80 Pfennigs
Nehmen Sie dieses Papier/diese Nummer.	Take this paper/number.
Gehen Sie zur Kasse.	Go to the cashier.
Dort wird man Ihnen das Geld geben.	They'll give you the money there.

das Geld	money	das Scheckbuch	check book
das Bargeld	cash	der Scheck	check
das Kleingeld	change	die Währung	currency
der Geldschein/ die Banknote	bill	das Konto	account
der 20-Mark-Schein	20-Mark bill	ein Konto eröffnen	to open an account
der Kassen-schalter	cashier's window	deponieren/ einzahlen	to deposit
zahlen	to pay	abheben	to withdraw

37

Persönlicher Ausweis (personal identification)

Ihren Paß, bitte.	Your passport, please.
Ohne einen Paß können wir Reisechecks nicht einlösen.	We can't cash traveler's checks without a passport.
Ich habe eine Scheckkarte	I have a check card
eine Kontokarte	a bank card
eine Kreditkarte	a credit card

USEFUL WORDS AND EXPRESSIONS

Er (der Paß) ist zu Hause!	It's at home!

Asking questions

Wer?	Who?	**Wie?**	How?	**Wann?**	When?
Was?	What?	**Wieviel?**	How much/many?	**Wo?**	Where?

Nationalities

Sprechen Sie langsam.	Speak slowly.
Ich spreche kaum Deutsch.	I speak very little German.
Ich spreche nur ein bißchen Deutsch.	I only speak a little German.
Ich habe kein Deutsch.	I don't speak German.
Ich verstehe Sie nicht.	I don't understand you.

Ich bin Engländerin.	**Ich wohne in England.**	**Ich spreche Englisch.**
I am an Englishwoman.	I live in England.	I speak English.
Ich bin Amerikaner.	**Ich wohne in New York.**	**Ich spreche Englisch.**
I am an American.	I live in New York.	I speak English.
deutsche Zeitungen	**australische Strände**	**schweizerische Küche**
German newspapers	Australian beaches	Swiss cooking

Countries and languages

Deutschland	**der Deutsche/die Deutsche**	**deutsch**
Germany	German (man/woman)	German (adj.)

the way it works

More prepositions

1   These prepositions are followed by nouns in the object case (i.e., **der** changes to **den** in the masculine singular): **bis** (until); **durch** (through); **für** (for); **gegen** (about, in return for, against); **ohne** (without); **um** (around, at).

2   You have seen how **der/die/das** change after the prepositions **mit, zu** and **in**. The following prepositions cause the same changes (i.e., **der** and **das** change to **dem**; **die** changes to **der**): **aus** (out of, from); **bei** (near, at the home of); **gegenüber*** (opposite); **nach** (after); **seit** (since).
*Note that with **gegenüber**, the noun comes before the preposition.

3   Some prepositions take either of the endings in (1) or (2) above, depending on whether there is any movement involved or implied (see p. 28), e.g.:
Er **geht** hinter **das** Café (movement)   Er **ist** hinter **dem** Café (no movement)
an (at, to); **auf** (on); **hinter** (behind); **in** (in); **neben** (beside); **über** (over); **unter** (under); **vor** (in front of); **zwischen** (between)

4   *Contractions*   Just as **in** + **das** can become **ins, von** + **dem** = **vom**, etc., other prepositions join with **der/die/das** to form contractions:

an + dem = **am**	an + das = **ans**
auf + das = **aufs**	bei + dem = **beim**
durch + das = **durchs**	für + das = **fürs**
hinter + das = **hinters**	über + das = **übers**

things to do

4.1 1   You see the sign "Sparkasse."
Is it **(a)** a bank   **(b)** a currency exchange   **(c)** a cashier?
2   You are looking for the exchange rate.
Is it **(a)** der Wechselkurs   **(b)** der Bankbeamte
(c) das Anschlagbrett?
3   The teller says to you: "Das macht fünfunddreißig Mark zehn Pfennig."
Is it **(a)** DM 25,10   **(b)** DM 53,20   **(c)** DM 35,10?
4   You want the teller to give you some change as well as bills. Do you ask for **(a)** das Kleingeld   **(b)** das Geld   **(c)** das Bargeld?

4.2   You go into a bank to change some money. See if you can talk to the teller in German:
1   Say you would like to change $50 into Marks.
2   Say you would like to cash a traveler's check.
3   Ask what the exchange rate is today.
4   Ask if you can cash a check. Say your passport is at the hotel, but you have a credit card.

BUYING STAMPS

Post Offices Monday through Friday German post offices are open 8 a.m. to 6 p.m., and 8 a.m. to Noon on Saturdays. In Austria they are open 8:00–5:00 and in Switzerland 7:30–6:30 p.m., with a break for lunch at noon. Post offices at train stations and in larger cities are open until later in the evening on weekdays.

Mailboxes are yellow (sometimes blue in Austria). Stamps can be bought from the post office, from vending machines outside post offices and telephone booths, and from stationery stores and newspaper stands.

einen Brief schicken/sending a letter

Postbeamter: Bitte schön, meine Damen?
Helen: **Wieviel kostet eine Postkarte nach England**, bitte?
Postbeamter: Siebzig Pfennig.
Helen: Und **was kostet ein Brief**?
Postbeamter: Nach England? Der kostet neunzig Pfennig.
Helen: Geben Sie mir bitte **fünf Briefmarken zu siebzig** und eine zu neunzig.
Postbeamter: Fünf Stück zu siebzig und eine zu neunzig, das sind zusammen . . .
Helen: Oh, und **ich muß auch eine Postkarte** in die Vereinigten Staaten **senden**.
Ulrike: Und **ich möchte dieses Paket** nach Freiburg **schicken**.
Postbeamter: Moment mal, meine Damen. Ich suche meinen Rechner!

Im Postamt (at the post office)

die Deutsche Bundespost	German Federal postal service
der Postbeamte	post office clerk
der Brief (pl. die Briefe)	letter
die Briefmarke/das Paket	stamp/package
Wieviel kostet eine Postkarte nach England, bitte:	How much is a postcard to England, please?
Was kostet ein Brief nach Italien?	How much is a letter to Italy?
Was kostet ein Paket nach Australien?	How much is a package to Australia?
Nach England? Das kostet neunzig Pfennig.	To England? That's 90 Pfennigs.
Geben Sie mir fünf Briefmarken zu ziebzig und eine zu neunzig	Give me 5 stamps at 70 Pf. and one at 90 Pf.
Fünf Stück zu siebzig . . .	Five at 70 Pf. . . .
Ich möchte eine Postkarte in die Vereinigten Staaten senden/schicken.	I'd like to send a postcard to the USA.
Ich möchte ein Paket nach Freiburg schicken	I'd like to send a package to Freiburg
per Luftpost/per Normaltarif	by air/by surface mail
per Einschreiben/per Expreß	registered/express mail
Was macht das?	How much is that?
Das sind zusammen . . .	Altogether that comes to . . .
Ich möchte eine Internationale Postanweisung einlösen.	I'd like to cash an international money order.
Ich möchte ein Telegramm aufgeben.	I'd like to send a telegram.
Wo ist der Briefkasten?	Where is the mail box?
das Postfach	post office box
Moment mal, meine Damen. Ich suche meinen Rechner.	Just a moment, ladies. I'm looking for my calculator.

POST/POSTAMT	post office
POSTWERT-ZEICHEN BRIEFMARKEN	} stamps
BRIEFMARKEN AUTOMAT	stamp vending machine
POSTLAGERNDE SENDUNG	general delivery
PAKETE	packages
TELEGRAMME	telegrams

Post

the way it works

Indirect object pronouns

1   Pronouns too change when following prepositions. You have already seen how they change after **für, ohne**, etc. This is how they change after **mit, zu, von**, etc. These pronouns are said to be in the indirect object, or dative case:

mit mir	with me	**mit uns**	with us
zu dir	to you		
von Ihnen	from you	**von Ihnen**	from you (pl.)
bei ihm/ihr	near him/her	**bei ihnen**	near them

41

2   Indirect object pronouns occur after certain verbs. In many cases, these are the same in English, e.g., **geben** (to give):

	indirect object	*direct object*
ich gebe	**ihr**	das Formular
I give	(to) her	the form

You will find indirect object pronouns after these verbs: bringen (to bring), schicken (to send), danken (to thank), sended (to send), geben (to give), zeigen (to show), helfen (to help).

More verbs

wollen *to want*		**sprechen** *to speak*	
ich **will**	wir **wollen**	ich **spreche**	wir **sprechen**
du **willst**	Sie **wollen**	du **sprichst**	Sie **sprechen**
Sie **wollen**		Sie **sprechen**	
er/sie/es **will**	sie **wollen**	er/sie/es **spricht**	sie **sprechen**

werden *to become*	
ich **werde**	wir **werden**
du **wirst**	Sie **werden**
Sie **werden**	
er/sie/es **wird**	sie **werden**

In the future

When talking about something that is going to happen in the future, use **werden** plus a verb in the infinitive, e.g.:

ich **werde fragen** (I will/shall ask)	wir **werden suchen** (we will look for)
du **wirst antworten** (you will answer)	Sie **werden geben** (you will give)
sie **wird kommen** (she will come)	sie **werden nehmen** (they will take)

His and her

In German, these are **sein** and **ihr**:

sein Bruder	his brother	**sein** Haus	his house
ihr Bruder	her brother	**ihr** Haus	her house
seine Tochter	his daughter	**seine** Kinder	his children
ihre Tochter	her daughter	**ihre** Kinder	her children

things to do

4.3 You are in a German post office.

1   First you want to know if any mail has arrived for you. What sign do you look for?

2   You want to send a letter to the United States. What do you ask the clerk?

3   You want to buy three stamps at 70 Pfennig. What do you say?

4   Say you would like to send a package to New York, and ask how much it comes to.

5   Say you would like to cash an international money order.

6   Ask how much it costs to send a postcard to Australia.

RENTING A CAR

Driving   Germany, Austria and Switzerland have many miles of highway
(**Autobahn**) and good secondary roads. Germany has 4,600 miles of
highways without tolls, Austria has some toll ways and in Switzerland
highway users must obtain special windshield stickers. There are road
service patrols on highways and major roads, and in Germany gas stations
and restaurants located near the highway often have displays of useful
information on that area.

When driving, seat belts must be worn, and children under 12 must travel
in the back of the car. Insurance is mandatory. Motorists must carry a red
warning triangle and a first-aid kit, and headlights must be dimmed when
driving in foggy conditions. Use headlights when driving at dusk. On
Alpine roads, snow tires and chains must be used in winter.

Car rental   There are car rental offices at over 40 main train stations in
Germany. Cars can also be delivered to airports and hotels. Rates vary from
place to place, and you may be charged by the kilometer or by the day. In
larger towns, chauffeur-driven transportation is also available.

bei der Autovermietung/at the car rental office

On Friday, George Jackson has a free morning. He rents a car in order to take Helen, Gisela, and Thomas out to the country.

George:	Guten Morgen. **Ich möchte ein Auto** mieten, bitte.
Angestellter:	Sicherlich. Für vier Personen? Wir haben einen mittleren Volkswagen, oder einen großen Audi mit Automatik. Der Audi hat auch ein Radio mit Kassettenrecorder.
George:	**Bezahlt man pro Tag oder pro Kilometer?**
Angestellter:	Es kommt darauf an . . .
Thomas:	Toll! Wieviel kostet der Audi?
Angestellter:	(handing George a form) Hier sind die Gebühren und die Versicherungskosten. Aber, entschuldigen Sie bitte, ist das Auto für den Herrn, oder wird dieser junge Mann auch fahren?
George:	(hastily) Nein, nein—nur ich. Also, **wir nehmen den VW**, danke.
Angestellter:	Zeigen Sie mir bitte Ihren Führerschein. (He checks the license) Alles ist in Ordnung, Herr Jackson. Hier ist der Schlüssel. Kommen Sie mit mir, wir sehen uns das Auto an . . .

Renting a car

die Autovermietung	car rental office
Ich möchte ein Auto/ein Wagen mieten.	I'd like to rent a car.
Für wie lange?	For how long?
Sicherlich. Für vier Personen?	Of course. For four?
Wir haben einen mittleren VW . . .	We have a medium-sized VW . . .
einen großen Audi	a large Audi
mit Automatik	automatic
Er hat ein Radio mit Kassettenrecorder.	It has a radio with a cassette player.
Bezahlt man pro Tag oder pro Kilometer?	Do you pay by the day or by the kilometer?
Wieviel kostet der Audi?	How much does the Audi cost?
Wieviel kostet es für einen Tag/eine Woche?	How much does it cost for a day/a week?
Hier sind die Gebühren und die Versicherungskosten.	Here are the rates and the insurance charges.
Muß ich eine Kautionssumme zahlen?	Do I have to leave a deposit?
Nein, wenn Sie mit einer Kreditkarte bezahlen, dann nicht.	No, not if you pay by credit card.
Kann ich den Wagen in Frankfurt lassen?	Can I leave the car in Frankfurt?
Wir nehmen den VW, danke.	We'll take the VW, thank you.

Zeigen Sie mir Ihren Führerschein.	Show me your driver's license.
Alles ist in Ordnung.	Everything is in order.
Hier ist der Schlüssel.	Here is the key.
Wir sehen uns das Auto an.	We'll take a look at the car.
die Vollkaskoversicherung	full insurance coverage
der Führerschein/die Autopapiere	driver's license/registration
Gute Fahrt!	Have a good trip!

On the road (auf den Weg)

das Auto	car	das Moped	moped
der Lastkraft- wagen (LKW)	truck	der Motorroller	scooter
		das Fahrrad	bicycle
der Wohnwagen	camper	der Verkehr	traffic
der Reisebus	bus	die Verkehrstauung	traffic jam
das Motorrad	motorcycle	die Geschwindig- kietsbegrenzung	speed limit
der Kleinbus	minibus		

DRIVING

Restrictions and breakdowns   Speed limits are 50 km/hr (32 mph) in built-up areas and villages (60 km/hr [38 mph] in Switzerland), and 100 (62) on all other roads except highways and divided highways. On German highways there are no limits, but 130 (82) is the recommended maximum speed. If you are stopped for speeding, you will have to produce your license and you may be fined on the spot. Breathalyzer tests are used and drinking and driving is a serious offense. If you are over the limit, you will lose your license immediately.

Traffic signs use international symbols and are easy to learn. In urban parking areas, parking stickers (**Parkscheiben**) can be bought from gas stations, tobacco shops and tourist offices.

Emergency telephones are situated along highways, and in Germany, the ADAC (**Allgemeiner Deutscher Automobil Club**) runs an emergency road service (**Straßenwachthilfe**). They also advise foreign motorists who are members of affiliated organizations, and publish maps and guidebooks.

At the gas station (an der Tankstelle)

die Tankstelle	gas station
Selbsttanken/Selbstbedienung.	self-service
Ich brauche Benzin.	I need some gas.
Super/Normal/Diesel/bleifreies Benzin	super/regular/diesel/lead-free gas
Fünfundzwanzig Liter Benzin, bitte.	25 liters of gas, please
Für zwanzig Mark Super.	20 Marks' worth of super.
Volltanken, bitte.	Fill it up, please.
Normal voll, bitte.	Fill it up with regular, please.
Bitte prüfen Sie . . .	Please check . . .
das Öl/das Wasser/die Reifen/die Batterie	the oil/water/tires/battery
den Reifendruck prüfen	check the tire pressure
Führen Sie Reparaturen aus?	Do you do repairs?

In town

Darf ich hier parken?	Can I park here?
die Parkuhr	parking meter
der Parkplatz	parking lot
die Hochgarage	parking garage
die Parkscheibe	parking sticker

eine Panne/a breakdown

George and the three young people stop at a village to admire the view, but unfortunately, the car seems to be giving them some trouble.

Thomas: Was ist los, Herr Jackson? Brauchen wir vielleicht Benzin?

George: (Trying to start the car) Himmel, **der Wagen springt nicht an!** (He tries again) Nein, **da ist etwas kaputt!** Gisela, dort drüben steht eine Telefonzelle. Rufen Sie sofort eine Reparaturwerkstatt an.

am Apparat/on the phone

Gisela: Hallo? Führen Sie Reparaturen aus? **Ich möchten den Mechaniker sprechen,** bitte.

Angestellte: Einen Augenblick, bitte . . . Das tut mir leid, er ist gerade nicht da.

Gisela: **Würden Sie bitte etwas ausrichten?** Mein Name ist Fräulein Bauer, und mein VW hat im Dorf eine Panne. Bitte schicken Sie sobald wie möglich den Mechaniker.

Angestellte: Danke. **Auf Wiederhören.**

46

At the garage (in der Reparaturwekstatt)

die Reparaturwerkstatt	repair garage
Ich habe einen Unfall gehabt.	I've had an accident.
Mein Auto hat eine Panne.	My car has broken down
Es steht zwei Kilometer von hier.	It's 2 km from here.
Ich habe kein Benzin mehr im Tank.	I've run out of gas.
Ich habe eine Reifenpanne.	I've got a flat tire.
Können Sie den Reifendruck prüfen?	Can you check the tire pressure?
Mein Wagen springt nicht an.	My car won't start.
Die Batterie ist leer.	The battery is dead.
Der Motor geht aus.	The engine stalls.
Schicken Sie sobald wie möglich einen Mechaniker.	Send a mechanic as soon as possible.
der Abschleppwagen	tow truck
der Anlasser/die Blinker	the starter/turn signals
. . . ist/sind nicht in Ordnung	. . . isn't/aren't working
. . . funktioniert/funktionieren nicht	. . . isn't/aren't working
(For a list of car parts, see p. 80)	
Können Sie mir bitte einen Kostenvoranschlag geben?	Can you give me an estimate, please?
Wann wird das Auto fertig sein?	When will the car be ready?

Road signs

AUTOBAHN	highway	**HALT**	stop
AUSFAHRT	exit	**MAUTSTELLE**	toll (Austria)
EINFAHRT	entrance	**UMLEITUNG**	detour
GEFAHR	danger	**VORSICHT**	careful
GRENZE	border		
GRENZ-KONTROLLE	customs inspection		

Bauarbeiten	roadwork
Blaue Zone	restricted parking zone
Durchfahrt verboten	no through traffic
Einbahnstraße	one-way street
Einordnen	get in the lane
Keine Einfahrt	no entry
Langsam fahren	drive slowly
Rechts fahren	keep to the right
Überholen verboten	no passing
Vorfahrt beachten	yield

Telephones   Both local and long-distance telephone calls can be made easily from phone booths (**Fernsprecher**) in Germany, Austria, and Switzerland. You will find that some public phones take coins, while an increasing number take special phone cards, called **Telefonkarte** in Germany or **Wertkarte** in Austria. These phone cards can be purchased at post offices and newsstands. In all of these countries, international calls made from a hotel can be subject to a large surcharge, so you can take advantage of public phones to save money. To call abroad, dial 00, then the country code, followed by the area code and the phone number.

George Jackson is checking in at the Hotel Berlin.

REZEPTION

George:	(to receptionist) Guten Abend. **Ich habe ein Zimmer reserviert—für eine Woche.**
Empfangsdame:	Guten Abend. Ihr Name, bitte?
George:	Mein Name ist Jackson.
Empfangsdame:	Einen Moment, bitte . . . Jackson . . . **ein Doppelzimmer, mit Bad** . . .
George:	Nein, **ein Einzelzimmer, mit Dusche!**
Empfangsdame:	Sie kommen aus Birmingham, Herr Jackson?
George:	Nein, ich komme aus London. (He shows the receptionist his confirmation receipt.) **Hier ist die Bestätigung.**
Empfangsdame:	Herr Jackson aus London. Ah, das stimmt—**Zimmer acht, im Erdgeschoß. Hier ist der Schlüssel.**
George:	Danke schön.
Empfangsdame:	Bitte schön.

Making a hotel reservation

Haben Sie Zimmer frei?	Do you have any rooms?
Mein Name ist . . .	My name is . . .
Ich habe ein Zimmer reserviert . . .	I have reserved a room . . .
für eine Nacht/drei Nächte	for one night/three nights
für eine Woche/zwei Wochen	for a week/two weeks
Ich möchte . . .	I would like . . .
ein Einzelzimmer	a single room
ein Doppelzimmer	a double room
ein Zimmer mit zwei Betten	a room with twin beds
mit Bad/mit Dusche	with a bath/shower
mit Toilette/mit Fernsehen	with toilet/with a TV
mit Telefon/mit Balkon	with a telephone/balcony
nach vorn/nach hinten	at the front/at the back
im Erdgeschoß	on the ground floor
im ersten Stock	on the second floor
im zweiten Stock	on the third floor
Für wieviele Personen?	For how many?
Für eine Person/Für zwei Personen	For one/For two
Vollpension/Halbpension	with/without meals
Übernachtung mit Frühstück	Bed and breakfast

PENSION
Roseneck
am Wald

HOTEL
ALTE
POST

Using the telephone

das Telefon	telephone
die Telefon- nummer	phone number
das Telefonbuch	directory
die Telefonzelle	phone booth
die Vorwähl- nummer	area code
das Amtszeichen	dial tone

die Vermittlung	operator
die Auskunft	information
eine Nummer wählen	dial a number
das Ortgespräch	local call
das Ausland- gespräch	international call

telefonieren/anrufen	to telephone
Wo kann ich telefonieren?	Where can I make a phone call?
Dort drüben steht eine Telefonzelle.	There's a phone booth over there.
Rufen Sie sofort eine Reparaturwerkstatt an.	Call a garage right away.
Ich brauche Münzen.	I need some coins.
Münzeinwurf/Münzrückgabe	Insert coins/coin return
Kann ich bitte ein Amt haben?	May I have a line please?
Hallo, hier Jackson.	Hello, this is Mr. Jackson.
Jackson am Apparat.	Mr. Jackson speaking.
Ich möchte den Mechaniker sprechen.	I'd like to speak to the mechanic.
Ich hätte gern Apparat hundertzwo*	I'd like extension 102
ein Gespräch mit Voranmeldung	a person-to-person call
ein R-Gespräch	a collect call
Wieviel kostet es?	How much does it cost?

*On the phone, use **zwo** not **zwei**

Understanding the reply

Wer ist am Apparat?	Who's speaking?
Einen Augenblick, bitte.	Just a moment, please.
Bitte warten Sie.	Please wait.
Ich verbinde Sie.	I'm connecting you.
Bleiben Sie am Apparat.	Stay on the line.
Es ist besetzt.	The line's busy.
Es antwortet niemand/keiner.	There's no answer.
Sie haben sich verwählt.	You've got the wrong number.
Das tut mir leid, er ist gerade nicht da.	I'm sorry, he's not here at the moment.
Würden Sie bitte später nochmal versuchen?	Do you want to try again later?
Danke, ich rufe wieder an.	Thanks, I'll call back.
Würden Sie bitte etwas ausrichten?	Could you take a message, please?
Meine Telefonnummer ist . . .	My phone number is . . .
Ich komme nicht durch.	I can't get through.
Ich bin unterbrochen worden.	I've been cut off.
Auf Wiederhören!	Goodbye!

USEFUL WORDS AND EXPRESSIONS

Es kommt darauf an . . .	It depends . . .
Toll!	Fantastic!
Wird dieser junge Mann auch fahren?	Will this young man be driving too?
Nur ich	Just me
Himmel!	Heavens!

the way it works

Verbs that separate

Some verbs in German separate into two parts when not in the infinitive, and the first part normally goes to the end of the sentence. Here are some examples:

ansehen to look at   Wir **sehen** das Auto **an**. (We look at the car.)
anspringen to start (engine)   Der Wagen **springt** nicht **an**. (The car doesn't start.)
anrufen to call, phone   **Rufen** Sie eine Reparaturwerkstatt **an**. (Call a garage.)
zurückkommen to come back   Der Mechaniker **kommt** um 8 Uhr **zurück**. (The mechanic is coming back at 8 o'clock.)
ausführen to carry out   Er **führt** die Reparaturen **aus**. (He does the repairs.)

More about adjectives

You may have noticed that when **der/die/das** are not mentioned, adjectives take these endings:

schwarz**er** Kaffee (m)   weiß**e** Limonade (f)   stark**es** Bier (n)

Adjectives that come before the noun change in the object case as follows:

	masc.	fem.	neuter
Ich sehe	den großen Audi	die kleine Tür	das alte Fahrrad
Wir haben	einen großen Audi	eine kleine Tür	ein altes Fahrrad

49

things to do

5.1 You are at a gas station in Germany.

  1 Ask for 30 liters of super.

  2 Ask if you can check the tire pressure.

  3 Ask if they can check the battery.

  4 Ask if they do repairs.

5.2 You are renting a car.

  1 Say you would like a small car.

  2 Ask how much it costs for 2 days.

  3 Ask if you have to leave a deposit.

  4 Say you want to leave the the car in Stuttgart.

  5 Say you'll take the blue Volkswagen and ask for the key.

5.3 **1** You are on the highway and looking for the exit. What sign do you look for?

  2 You see the sign **EINBAHNSTRAßE**. Does it mean **(a)** no through traffic **(b)** one-way street **(c)** pedestrians only?

  3 You need to buy a parking sticker. Is it **(a)** ein Parkuhr **(b)** eine Parkscheibe **(c)** einen Parkplatz?

5.4 **A** Helen answers the phone at the Bauer's house. What does she say?

Frau Schott:	Hallo, bist du es, Ulrike?
Helen:	[No, this is Helen Jackson.]
Frau Schott:	Oh, entschuldigen Sie. Hier Frau Schott—darf ich Frau Bauer sprechen?
Helen:	[Wait a moment . . . I'm sorry, she's not here.]
Frau Schott:	Wann kommt sie wieder zurück?
Helen:	[She's coming back at half past five, I think.]
Frau Schott:	Danke, ich versuche später nochmal.
Helen:	[Goodbye.]

  B Now Helen tries to call Thomas at his apartment, but he doesn't seem to be there. Günther answers the phone.

Günther:	Hallo, hier Günther Rascher.
Helen:	[I'd like to speak to Thomas, please.]
Günther:	Leider is er gerade nicht da. Wer ist am Apparat, bitte?
Helen:	[It's Helen Jackson speaking.]
Günther:	Ach so. Wollen Sie eine Nachricht für ihn hinterlassen?
Helen:	[No, I'll call back later.]
Günther:	Gut. Auf Wiederhören.
Helen:	[Goodbye.]

HEALTH PROBLEMS

Health You might wish to purchase traveler's insurance before leaving for Europe. Check with your insurance agent. Pharmacists may sell and recommend medicine that is often only available in the U.S. by prescription. If you take prescription medicine, always carry your prescription with you.

Doctor's office hours are normally 10 a.m. to noon and 4 p.m. to 6 p.m. (except weekends and Wednesdays).

ein Unfall/an accident

Nach dem Mittagessen machen die jungen Leute einen kurzen Spaziergang in das Dorf. George aber bleibt im Auto und hört Radio. *(After lunch, the youngsters go for a short walk into the village. However, George stays in the car and listens to the radio.)*

Helen:	Die Landschaft ist sehr schön—aber wo ist Thomas?
Eine Stimme:	Hilfe!
Gisela:	(running up) Thomas, was ist los?
Thomas:	**Ich bin hingefallen** . . .
Gisela:	Bist du verletzt? Wo hast du Schmerzen?

51

Thomas:	Ach, **ich kann den Fuß nicht bewegen. Er tut mir weh! Mein Knöchel ist gebrochen,** glaube ich.
Helen:	Ja, **der Fuß ist sehr geschwollen.** Guck mal die große blaue Quetschung!
Gisela:	Er muß vielleicht ins Krankenhaus!

(Back at the car)

George:	Lassen Sie mich sehen, junger Mann.
Thomas:	Ah, vorsichtig!
George:	So, das ist sicherlich eine Muskelzerrung. Gibt es eine Apotheke in diesem Dorf? Der Apotheker wird uns beraten.

Bei der Apotheke (At the pharmacy)

Gisela:	Es ist ein Unfall passiert. Mein Bruder hat große Schmerzen im Knöchel.
Apotheker:	Wie fühlen Sie sich?
Thomas:	**Schlecht. Mir ist schwindlig.**
Helen:	Hat er Fieber?
Apotheker:	Nein, die Temperatur ist nicht hoch. Machen Sie sich keine Sorgen, das ist nichts Ernstes. Nehmen Sie dieses Schmerzmittel, und ruhen Sie sich aus.
Gisela:	**Wieviel** soll er **einnehmen?**
Apotheker:	**Zwei Tabletten, dreimal am Tag.**
Thomas:	Nein, nein, keine Droge für mich. Heutzutage nehme ich nur homöopathische Mittel!

Seeking medical attention

(A list of parts of the body is given on p. 81.)

Was ist los?	What's the matter?/What's up?
Ich bin hingefallen.	I fell.
Bist du verletzt?	Are you hurt?
Ich habe Schmerzen.	I'm in pain.
Ich bin krank.	I'm ill.
der Arzt/das Krankenhaus	doctor/hospital
die Krankenschwester	nurse
die Röntgenaufnahme	X ray
die Sprechstunden	office hours
Ich brauche einen Arzt.	I need a doctor.
Wo ist die nächste Arztpraxis?	Where is the nearest doctor's office?
Ich möchte einen Termin.	I'd like an appointment.
Ich bin angemeldet.	I have an appointment.
der ärztliche Notdienst	emergency service

Explaining what's wrong

Mein(e) . . . tut weh.	My . . . hurts.
Wo hast du Schmerzen?	Where does it hurt?
Ich kann den Fuß nicht bewegen.	I can't move my foot.
Mein Knöchel ist geschwollen/ gebrochen/verstaucht.	My ankle is swollen/broken/sprained.
Mein Bruder hat große Schmerzen im Knöchel.	My brother has a bad pain in his ankle.
Guck mal die große blaue Quetschung!	Look at the big blue bruise!
Vorsichtig!	Be careful!
Es tut mir weh.	It hurts.
Ich habe etwas im Auge.	I've got something in my eye.
Ich habe mir die Hand verbrannt.	I've burned my hand.
Ich bin gestochen/gebissen worden.	I've been stung/bitten.
Ich kann nicht schlafen/atmen.	I can't sleep/breathe.
Ich habe mich übergeben/ich habe erbrochen.	I've been vomiting.
Ich habe Magenschmerzen Kopfschmerzen/Ohrenschmerzen Husten/Halsschmerzen Durchfall	I have stomach ache a headache/earache a cough/sore throat diarrhea
Ich bin Diabetiker/Asthmatiker.	I'm diabetic/asthmatic.
Ich bin herzkrank.	I have heart trouble.
Ich bin gegen Penizillin allergisch.	I'm allergic to penicillin.
Ich bin schwanger.	I'm pregnant.
Ich nehme die Pille.	I'm on the pill.
Keine Droge für mich.	No drugs for me.
Heuzutage nehme ich nur homöopathische Mittel.	These days I only take homeopathic remedies.
Lassen Sie mich sehen.	Let me see.
Wie fühlen Sie sich?	How do you feel?
Schlecht. Mir ist schwindlig.	Bad. I feel dizzy.
Ich fühle mich nicht wohl.	I don't feel well.
Hat er Fieber?	Does he have a temperature?
Die Temperatur ist nicht hoch.	His temperature isn't high.
Das ist sicherlich eine Muskelzerrung.	That's surely a torn muscle.
Er muß vielleicht ins Krankenhaus.	Perhaps he'll have to go to the hospital.
Sie müssen im Bett bleiben.	You must stay in bed.
Sie brauchen eine Spritze/einen Bluttest.	You need an injection/a blood test.
Machen Sie sich keine Sorgen.	Don't worry.
Das ist nichts Ernstes.	It's not serious.

Pharmacies   Business hours are 9 a.m. to 6 p.m., Monday through Friday and until 2 p.m. on Saturday. An **Apotheke** (recognizable by the sign of a red A) is a pharmacy, whereas a **Drogerie** is similar to a drugstore. The pharmacist will give you helpful advice, first aid treatment, or refer you to a doctor if necessary. Details of pharmacists' rotation system for nights (**NACHTSDIENST**) and Sundays (**SONNTAGDIENST**) are posted on the door of the shop.

At the pharmacy bei der Apotheke)

(For a list of items at the pharmacy, see p. 78)

die Apotheke	pharmacy
dienstbereite Apotheken	pharmacists on rotation
die Drogerie	drugstore
Wo ist die nächste Apotheke?	Where is the nearest chemist's?
Gibt es eine Apotheke in diesem Dorf?	Is there a pharmacy in this village?
Der Apotheker wird uns beraten.	The pharmacist will advise us.
Geben Sie mir bitte . . .	Please give me . . .

Minor problems

Ich habe Insektenstiche/Heufieber Reisekrankheit//Sonnenbrand.	I have insect bites/hay fever travel sickness/sunburn.
Ich nehme dieses Medikament.	I take this medicine.
Ich brauche etwas/Tabletten gegen . . .	I need something/pills for . . .
Ich habe ein Rezept.	I have a prescription.
Nehmen Sie dieses Schmerzmittel.	Take this painkiller.
Wieviel soll ich einnehmen?	How many should I take?
Zwei Tabletten, dreimal am Tag.	Two tablets three times a day.
einmal, zweimal	once, twice
alle vier Stunden/täglich/stündlich	every four hours/daily/hourly
vor/nach dem Essen	before/after meals
Keine Droge für mich.	No drugs for me.
Ruhen Sie sich aus.	Rest yourself.

At the dentist's (bei dem Zahnarzt)

der Zahnarzt	dentist
Ich habe Zahnschmerzen	I've got a toothache
wundes Zahnfleisch	sore gums
Ich habe eine Füllung verloren.	I've lost a filling.
Dieser Zahn ist abgebrochen.	This tooth is broken.

OTHER EMERGENCIES

Problems   If disaster strikes, go to the police station (**Polizeiwache**), the embassy, or ask for help at the hotel. *Wichtige Rufnummer* (important numbers): for the police, dial 110 (Germany); 133 (Austria); 117 (Switzerland).

Disasters

Hilfe!	Help!	**Gefahr!**	Danger!
Polizei!	Police!	**Feuer!**	Fire!
Notausgang	Emergency Exit	**Vorsicht**	Caution
Bergwacht	Mountain rescue	**Schwimmweste**	Lifejacket
Rettungsdienst	Rescue/ambulance	**Rettungsgürtel**	Lifebelt
		Feuerlöscher	Fire extinguisher

Holen Sie Hilfe!	Get help!
Wo ist die Polizeiwache?	Where is the police station
das Krankenhaus?	hospital?
Es ist ein Unfall passiert.	There's been an accident.
Rufen Sie bitte die Polizei	Call the police
die Feuerwehr/einen Arzt	the fire department/a doctor
einen Krankenwagen	an ambulance
Erste Hilfe	First aid

Der Autounfall (car accident)

Ich habe Vorfahrt gehabt.	I had right of way.
Es war Ihre Schuld.	It was your fault.
die Versicherungsgesellschaft	insurance company
einen Unfall melden	to report an accident
der Verletzte/die Geldstrafe	casualty/fine
die Blutprobe	blood test (for alcohol)

Loss and theft

Ich habe meinen Schlüssel verloren	I've lost my key
meinen Paß/meinen Fotoapparat	my passport/my camera/
meine Karte	my ticket
Man hat meine Handtasche gestohlen	Someone's stolen my handbag
mein Portemonnaie/meine	my purse/my wallet
Brieftasche	
Ich habe mich verirrt.	I'm lost.
das Konsulat/die Botschaft	consulate/embassy
das Fundamt	lost and found

USEFUL WORDS AND EXPRESSIONS

Die Landschaft is sehr schön.	The countryside is very pretty.

the way it works

Expressions with mir and Ihnen

In German, it is common to use **mir** (to me) when talking about how you're feeling:

Wie geht es **Ihnen**?	How are you?
Mir ist schlecht.	I don't feel well.
Mir ist schwindlig.	I feel dizzy.
Mir is kalt.	I feel cold.

Notice also these expressions:

Es tut mir weh!	It hurts!
Es tut mir leid	I'm sorry
Wie gefällt es Ihnen?	How do you like it?
Mir ist das gleich/egal.	It's all the same to me.

Something good, nothing serious . . .

In these expressions, the words for "good," "serious," etc. take a capital letter and the ending **-es**:

etwas Gut**es**	something good	etwas Interessant**es**	something interesting
nichts Ernst**es**	nothing serious	nichts Neu**es**	nothing new

Reflexive pronouns

Wie fühlen Sie **sich**?	How are you feeling?
Ich ruhe **mich** aus.	I'm resting.

The **sich** and **mich** in these sentences correspond roughly to "yourself," "myself," and are known as reflexive pronouns, as they reflect the actions of the speaker. Many verbs can be reflexive or non-reflexive, e.g.:

Ich wasche den Audi	I wash the Audi	(non-reflexive)
Ich wasche **mich**.	I wash myself.	(reflexive)

Here is the full list of reflexive pronouns:

sich entschuldigen to excuse oneself

ich **entschuldige mich** (I excuse myself)	wir **entschuldigen uns**
du **entschuldigst dich**	Sie **entschuldigen sich**
er/sie/es **entschuldigt sich**	sie **entschuldigen sich**

Some more verbs

tun to do		**dürfen** to be allowed, (may)	
ich **tue** (I do)	wir **tun**	ich **darf** (I may)	wir **dürfen**
du **tust**	Sie **tun**	du **darfst**	Sie **dürfen**
er/sie/es **tut**	sie **tun**	er/sie/es **darf**	sie **dürfen**

sollen shall, ought to, should	
ich **soll** (I shall)	wir **sollen**
du **sollst**	Sie **sollen**
er/sie/es **soll**	sie **sollen**

Like **können** and **müssen**, **dürfen** and **sollen** are *modal verbs,* and are used very frequently in German, followed by the infinitive. Examples: Darf man hier rauchen? Was soll ich tun?

things to do

5.5 Wo haben sie Schmerzen

5.6 **1** Your knee is sprained. Is it
   (a) verstaucht   **(b)** verbrannt   **(c)** gebrochen?
2 You fell sick and decide to consult the pharmacist.
   (a) Ask where the nearest pharmacy is.
   (b) Say you have vomited and ask if the pharmacist has
       something for a stomachache.
   (c) Say you have burned your finger and you would like some
       painkillers. Ask if you need a prescription.
   (d) Ask how often (**wie oft**) you should take the tablets.
   (e) Say you would also like some antiseptic and some cotton
       balls.

5.7 **Im Notfall . . .** (In an emergency . . .)
1 You have lost your traveler's checks. What do you say?
   (a) Ich habe meine Reiseschecks verloren.
   (b) Ich habe meine Kreditkarten verloren.
   (c) Ich habe meine Scheckkarten verloren.
2 Your luggage has been stolen. What do you tell the police?
   (a) Man hat meinen Rucksack gestohlen.
   (b) Man hat meine Reisetasche gestohlen.
   (c) Man hat mein Gepäck gestohlen.
3 You have left your tickets at the hotel. How do you explain?
   (a) Ich habe meine Tabletten im Hotel gelassen.
   (b) Ich habe meine Karten im Hotel gelassen.
   (c) Ich habe meine Brille im Hotel gelassen.

5.8 *Sie und Ihre Gesundheit* (You and your health)
Read this advertisement for an item which can be obtained from the
pharmacy. Can you say what it is?

> Schlafen Sie gut! *Ruhnox* ist das Naturrezept gegen Schlaflosigkeit.
> Ein Mittel, so alt wie die Menschheit, frisch aus der Natur, *Ruhnox*
> beruhigt die Nerven und fördert einen guten Schlaf, ohne jede
> Chemie. Hilft auch bei Nervosität und innerer Unruhe. Packung
> mit 50 Dragees, in Apotheken und Drogerien.

so alt wie	as old as	**jede**	every, all
die Menschheit	mankind	**die Unruhe**	restlessness

LEISURE AND SPORTS

▶▶▶ **Sports** Sports are very popular, and all large towns have stadiums, swimming pools, etc. Horse racing and riding are enjoyed in Germany, along with golf, tennis and fishing in the inland waterways. Soccer is extremely popular in Germany, Austria and Switzerland. Cycling is becoming increasingly popular, and in Germany bicycles can be rented at over 200 train stations in tourist areas. The skiing season runs from November to April and attracts visitors from all over the world. Skating and ice hockey are also favorite winter pastimes.

im Sportzentrum/at the gym

It is late Saturday morning, and Helen goes with Gisela, Thomas and Karl-Heinrich to visit the gym.

Gisela: (proudly) Man kann hier im Sportzentrum an vielen verschiedenen Sportarten teilnehmen—es gibt Basketball, Handball, Schwimmen in der Schwimmhalle . . . normalerweise spielt der Thomas samstags Fußball, aber weil er verletzt ist, muß er heute Zuschauer sein, der Arme! Der Karl-Heinrich nimmt auch jede Woche Unterricht im Tennis. Wir haben hier herrliche Tennisplätze.

Thomas: Tennis ist ein blöder Sport . . .
Gisela: (continuing) Es gibt ein Radsport-stadion und eine
          Eissporthalle. Der Wintersport ist in Deutschland sehr populär.
Helen: **Ich möchte gern Schlittschuhlaufen,** Gisela. **Kann man hier
          Schlittschuhe leihen?**
Gisela: Ja, ja . . . Skier, Skistöcke, alles, was man für den Wintersport
          braucht.
Thomas: Heute mittag findet ein Fußballspiel im Stadion statt. **Ich
          möchte das Spiel gern sehen!**
Gisela: Toll—wir treffen uns um sechzehn Uhr zu Hause wieder. Aber
          Karl-Heinrich, du siehst sehr ärgerlich aus. Was ist denn los?
Karl-H.   Du weißt, daß ich nicht gern Tennis spiele. **Ich will** auch **zum
          Fußball gehen** . . .

Im Sportzentrum (at the gym)

(For a list of sports, see p. 80)

Ich treibe gern Sport.	I like sports.
Ich spiele gern Fußball.	I like playing soccer.
Mir gefällt das Schwimmen.	I like swimming.
Man kann an vielen verschiedenen Sportarten teilnehmen.	One can take part in many different sports.
Es gibt viele Gelegenheiten.	There are many facilities.
Es gibt Basketball, Handball . . .	There's basketball, handball . . .
Schwimmen in der Schwimmhalle	swimming in the pool
Es gibt ein Radsport-stadion und eine Eissporthalle	There's a cycling stadium and an ice rink
Normalerweise spielt der Thomas Fußball.	Thomas normally plays soccer.
weil er verletzt ist	since he's injured
Muß er Zuschauer sein, der Arme!	He'll have to be a spectator, the poor thing!
Heute mittag findet ein Spiel im Stadion statt.	There's a game this afternoon at the stadium.
Ich möchte gern das Spiel sehen.	I'd love to see the game.
Ich will zum Fußball gehen.	I want to go to the soccer game.
Karl-Heinrich nimmt Unterricht im Tennis.	Karl-Heinrich is taking tennis lessons.
Wir haben herrliche Tennisplätze.	We have lovely tennis courts.

Tennis ist ein blöder/herrlicher/ gesunder Sport.	Tennis is a stupid/fine/healthy sport.
Du weißt, das ich nicht gern Tennis spiele.	You know I don't like playing tennis.
Der Wintersport ist sehr populär.	Winter sports are very popular.
Ich möchte gern Schlittschuhlaufen	I'd love to go skating
Kann man Schlittschuhe leihen?	Can one rent skates?
Wievel kostet es pro Stunde/ pro Tag?	How much does it cost per hour/ per day?
Ich brauche Skier/Skistöcke	I need skis/ski poles
Alles, was man für den Wintersport braucht!	All you need for the winter sports!

USEFUL WORDS AND EXPRESSIONS

jede Woche	every week
Wir treffen uns zu Hause wieder.	We'll meet again at home.
Du siehst sehr ärgerlich aus	You look very angry.
Was ist denn los?	What's up?

the way it works

Word order in more complicated sentences

Sometimes a sentence is made up of more than one clause. If the clauses are joined together by **und** (and) or **aber** (but), then both are main clauses and the word order is not affected:

Thomas ist verletzt, **und** er muß Zuschauer sein.
Karl-Heinrich nimmt Unterricht im Tennis, **aber** er will zum Fußball.

In many sentences however, there is one main clause and one or more secondary (subordinate) clauses. In subordinate clauses, the word order is changed and the verb goes to the end of the clause:

Thomas muß Zuschauer sein, **weil** er verletzt **ist**.
Gisela fragt den Karl-Heinrich, **warum** er ärgerlich **ist**.

As the main verb must always be the second idea in any sentence, note the word order when a subordinate clause comes first:

Weil er verletzt **ist**, muß Thomas Zuschauer **sein**.

Listen for these words which will often introduce a subordinate clause:

als	when (in the past)	**warum**	why
weil	because, since	**wann**	when
da	since	**wie**	how, as
wenn	when, whenever, if	**wo**	where
ob	whether	**was**	that, which
daß	that		

Clauses are always separated by a comma in German:
Alles, was man für den Wintersport braucht.
Du weißt, daß ich nicht gern Tennis spiele.

SAMSTAG SATURDAY

To know

Wissen means "to know" and is used for knowing facts, abstract ideas, etc.:
Du weißt, daß ich samstags Fußball spiele.
You know (that) I play soccer on Saturdays.
Wissen Sie, wo mein Schläger ist?
Do you know where my racquet is?

Here is the verb in full:

ich **weiß**	I know	wir **wissen**	we know
du **weißt**	you know	Sie **wissen**	you know
er/sie/es **weiß**	he/she/it knows	sie **wissen**	they know

things to do

6.1 Match up the items in the two columns to make sentences:

1	Im Freibad	**(a)**	findet ein Fußballspiel statt.
2	Auf der Eisbahn	**(b)**	gibt es einen Sessellift.
3	Im Stadion	**(c)**	kann man baden gehen.
4	Auf den Skigeländen	**(d)**	sieht man Fahrräder.
5	Im Radsport-stadion	**(e)**	spielt man Golf.
6	Am Golfplatz	**(f)**	geht man Schlittschuhlaufen.

6.2 1 You need to rent some hiking equipment. Do you ask for:

(a) die Schneebrille

(b) den Taucheranzug

(c) die Wandrausrüstung?

2 You need skis, ski boots, ski poles and a lift ticket. Which can you *not* get from this shop?

Hier bekommen Sie Ihre

*★SKIER
SKISTIEFEL★
★LIFTPÄSSE*

6.3

CLUB D-SPORT *Wenn Sie sich körperlich fit halten wollen!*	
Eintrittspreise (Erwachsene über 18 Jahre)	
Hallenbad (4 Stunden)	16,- DM
Schwimmbad mit Sauna (ganztägig)	19,- DM
Trainings-Raum	9,50 DM
Teilmassage	15,- DM
Solarium 10 Minuten	2,- DM
Bringen Sie Ihre Familie, Freunde und Bekannten mit!	

ganztägig   all day   **Bekannte**   acquaintance

1 According to the chart, how much do you pay for the swimming session only?

2 What can you get for 2 Marks?

3 Who do the advertisers suggest you bring with you?

ENTERTAINMENT

▶▶▶ **Things to do**   Movie theaters, concert halls and theaters are in all large towns. Many also have opera houses, some of which are world famous. You will find night clubs, cafés and bars with live music (and **Bierkellers** in the south). In Hamburg and Berlin, there is virtually nonstop entertainment.

You are expected to dress fairly formally for the opera, casinos, the theater and some restaurants. In the theater, coats, umbrellas, etc. should be deposited in the cloakroom (**Garderobe**), and the attendant will expect a small tip. Generally, smoking is not permitted. Movie theaters usually have separate showings and tickets can be reserved in advance. It is not necessary to tip movie theater ushers.

Museums are normally open from 9 a.m. to 5 p.m. Most are closed on Mondays (a few close on Saturdays or Sundays).

wohin heute abend?/where shall we go tonight?

It is early evening, and the Bauer family is planning an outing.

Gisela: Was gibt's heute abend zu tun?
Ulrike: Vielleicht gibt es ein neues Stück im Theater?

Thomas	**Ich möchte gern einen Film sehen.** Im Kino 'Royal' am Karlsplatz läuft ein französischer Film mit Untertiteln.
Helen:	**Was ist das für ein Film**, eine Komödie?
Thomas:	Ich glaube schon—oder ein Krimi.
Ulrike	**Ich höre lieber ein gutes Konzert.** Hören Sie gern Musik, Helen? (looking at the paper) Im Staatstheater spielt man eine Mozart-Oper. Das wäre sehr schön!
Gisela:	Mir ist Oper zu langweilig. (looks at her watch) **Um wieviel Uhr beginnt der Film?**
Thomas:	Die Spätvorstellung fängt um zehn Uhr an und ist um halb eins zu Ende. Im 'Royal' kann man Plätze reservieren.
Gisela:	Prima! **Gehen wir erst in eine Diskothek.** Ich will heute abend tanzen gehen!

in einem bayerischen Bierkeller/in a Bavarian ale-house

George and Ernst stop in at "Zum Fässchen" for a drink after a hard day's work at the trade fair.

George:	Es ist sehr gemütlich hier.
Ernst:	Ja, und **samstags abends spielt man Jazz.** Interessieren Sie sich für Musik, George?
George:	Ja, besonders für Jazz. Kennen Sie den berühmten amerikanischen Saxophonisten? . . . ich habe den Namen vergessen. Wir haben ihn letztes Jahr in London gehört. Es war wirklich wunderbar.
Ernst:	Ich habe großen Durst. Was trinken Sie gern?
George:	In einem Münchner Bierkeller trinkt man natürlich ein gutes Münchner Bier!

Was gibt's heute zu tun? (What is there to do today?)

die Veranstaltungen	events
(For a list of entertainment, see p. 81.)	
Ich möchte zum Kino gehen.	I'd like to go to the movie theater.
Ich habe Lust, einen Film zu sehen.	I'd like to see a movie.
Ich möchte ein Konzert hören.	I'd like to go to a concert.
Ich würde gern das Museum besuchen.	I'd like to go to the museum.
Wann wird die Kunstgalerie geöffnet?	When does the gallery open?
Wann schließt das Museum?	When does the museum close?
Wieviel kostet die Eintrittskarte?	How much is the admission?

ÖFFNUNGSZEITEN	business hours	EINTRITT FREI	free admission
GEÖFFNET	open	GESCHLOSSEN	closed
RUHETAG	day off	FOTOGRAFIEREN VERBOTEN	no photographs

Movies and theater

Was gibt es heute im Kino zu sehen?/ Was läuft heute im Kino?	What's playing today?
Vielleicht gibt es ein neues Stück im Theater.	Perhaps there's a new play at the theater.
Im Kino läuft ein französischer Film.	There's a French film playing.
mit Untertiteln/synchronisiert	with subtitles/dubbed
Was für ein Film/Stück is das?	What kind of film/play is it?
eine Komödie/ein Trauerspiel/ein Krimi	a comedy/a tragedy/a thriller
ein Wildwestfilm/ein Zeichentrickfilm	a Western/a cartoon
das neues Stück/der neue Film von . . . wird im Theater gespielt/läuft im Kino	. . . 's new play/film is at the theater/ movie theater

Concert, opera, ballet

Ich höre lieber ein gutes Konzert.	I'd rather go to a good concert.
Hören Sie gern Musik?	Do you like listening to music?
Interessieren Sie sich für Musik?	Are you interested in music?
Im Staatstheater spielt man eine Mozart-Oper.	There's a Mozart opera at the State Theater.
Mir ist Oper zu langweilig.	Opera bores me.
samstags spielt man Jazz	on Saturdays they have jazz
Kennen Sie den berühmten amerikanischen Saxophonisten?	Do you know the famous American saxophonist?
Wir haben ihn in London gehört.	We heard him in London.
Es war wirklich wunderbar.	It was really wonderful.
Ich will tanzen gehen.	I want to go dancing.

Reserving tickets

Um wieviel Uhr beginnt die Vorstellung?	What time does the performance begin?
Sie fängt um 10 Uhr an.	It starts at 10 o'clock.
die Theateraufführung	theatrical performance
die Nachmittagsvorstellung	matinée
die Spätvorstellung	late-night showing
durchgehende Vorstellung	continuous performance
Wie lange dauert es?	How long does it last?
Um wieviel Uhr ist der Film zu Ende?	What time does the film end?
Die Vorstellung endet um viertel vor neun.	The performance ends at a quarter to nine.
Wieviel kostet der Eintritt?	How much are the tickets?
Wie teuer?	What price range?
Kann ich Plätze reservieren?	Can I reserve seats?
Es tut mir leid, es gibt keine Plätze mehr.	I'm sorry, there aren't any seats left.
Gibt es eine Ermäßigung für . . .	Is there a discount for . . .
Kinder/Studenten/Gruppen	children/students/groups
Rentner/Behinderte/Arbeitslose?	retirees/disabled/unemployed?

Buying a ticket

die Vorverkaufsstelle	box office
Zweimal Parkett, bitte.	Two orchestra seats, please.
Drei Plätze im ersten/zweiten Rang.	Three seats in the first/second balcony.
Einen Platz im Balkon.	One ticket in the balcony.
nach vorn/nach hinten	in the front/in the back

Likes and dislikes

Es gefällt mir.	I like it.
Es gefällt mir nicht.	I don't like it.
Die Musik gefällt mir.	I like the music.
Ich finde das interessant/langweilig.	I find it interesting/boring.
Ich habe deutsche Filme gern.	I like German films.
Ich habe russisches Ballet nicht gern.	I don't like the Russian ballet.
Ich kann Oper nicht leiden.	I hate opera.
Ich kann Jazz nicht ausstehen.	I can't stand jazz.

USEFUL WORDS AND EXPRESSIONS

Ich glaube schon.	I think so.
Das wäre schön!	That would be lovely!
Prima!	Great!
Es ist sehr gemütlich hier.	It's very nice here.
besonders	especially
Ich habe den Namen vergessen.	I've forgotten the (his) name.
in einem Münchner Bierkeller	in a Munich pub.

the way it works

Verbs with vowel changes

These verbs used in the dialogue have vowel changes for the parts that go with **er, sie** and **es**:

laufen: Im Kino **läuft** ein französischer Film
There's a French film at . . .

anfangen: Er **fängt** um 8 Uhr an.
It starts at 8 o'clock.

Other verbs with a similar vowel change are:

waschen (to wash): sie **wäscht**
fallen (to fall) es **fällt**

Word order

In a German sentence, use this order of words or phrases: **wann, wie, wo** (when, how, where):

Wir gehen **um elf Uhr zu Fuß ins Hotel zurück**.
We're going back to the hotel on foot at 11 o'clock.

Recognizing the past tense

You may have noticed in *Freitag* some examples of verbs used in the past tense:

Ich **habe** meine Karten **verloren**.
I have lost my tickets.

Man **hat** meine Brieftasche gestohlen.
Someone has stolen my wallet.

You will see from these that **haben** is used together with a part of the verb known as a **past participle**, which goes to the end of the sentence.

Many verbs form their past participles by adding **ge-** to the infinitive and substituting **-t** for the **-en** ending, e.g.:

machen: ich habe **ge**macht (I made, I have made)
sagen: ich habe **ge**sagt (I said . . .)
hören: ich habe **ge**hört (I heard . . .)

Some verbs do not appear to change, e.g.

vergessen: ich habe **vergessen** (I forgot, I have forgotten)
bekommen: ich habe **bekommen** (I got, I have got)

Many verbs change quite radically, e.g.:

bringen (bring): ich habe **gebracht**
helfen (help): ich habe **geholfen**

denken (think): ich habe **gedacht**
verstehen (understand): **verstanden**

With some verbs, especially verbs of motion, **sein** is used instead of **haben** to make the past tense:

kommen: ich **bin gekommen** (I came)
fahren: er **ist gefahren** (he drove)

gehen: Sie **sind gegangen** (you went)
bleiben: du **bist geblieben** (you stayed)

Listen for **ich hatte** (I had), **ich war** (I was).

To know

Kennen also means "to know," but is used for knowing people and places:

Kennen Sie den amerikanischen Saxophonist**en**?*
Do you know the American saxophonist?

Kennen Sie meine Eltern?
Do you know my parents?

Ich **kenne** München sehr gut!
I know Munich very well!

*Some masculine nouns add an **n** or **en** in the object case.

things to do

6.4

NEUERÖFFNUNGEN: *Zum Schwarzen Storch* die Discothek für jedermann! ★	Täglich geöffnet ☆ Im Herzen der Stadt ☆ Ab 20.00 Uhr Goethestr. gegenüber Hotel `Münchner Hof´

1   When was this
    night club opened?

2   Where is it located?

3   When and at what time is
    it open?

6.5

Was möchten sie heute tun?
Can you say what each of these people wants to do today? e.g.:
1   Er hat Lust, zum Theater zu gehen.

6.6   **A**

> ***GROSSER SAAL***   *19.30 Uhr   Samstag 3. Oktober*
> *Radio-Sinfonie-Orchester Frankfurt*   *Dirigent: Eliahu Inbal*
> *Großes Operettenkonzert mit Musik von Lehar, Offenbach und Strauß*
> *Balkon DM 20,-   Parkett DM 40,-*

B

> ***DEUTSCHES KUNSTINSTITUT***
> *Städtische Galerie*
> *Eintrittspreis: 3,00 DM*
> *öffnungszeiten: Dienstag bis Sonntag von 11.00 bis 18.00 Uhr*

C

> *Das Deutsche Künstlerische Kino präsentiert:*
> *neue Kürz-Filme aus Westdeutschland*
> *seit 6. Juni*

A   You want to reserve seats for this concert.
   1   Ask what time it ends.
   2   Ask if there are discounts for students.
   3   Say you'd like 2 tickets in the front of the balcony.

B   A German colleague calls to ask about the art gallery, of which
       you have details.
   1   Tell him how much it costs to get in.
   2   Tell him when the gallery is open.
   3   Tell him on which day it is closed.

C   You are interested in the films advertized.
   1   Ask what time the show begins.
   2   Ask if you can reserve seats.
   3   Ask for an orchestra seat ticket.

CAMPING AND VACATIONS

Camping   Camping is very popular and is highly organized, especially in Germany, where overnight youth hostel stays and hiking are also favorite activities. There are hundreds of official campgrounds, many in picturesque areas—in the mountains or lakeside (details from the National Tourist Offices, the motor clubs and the various published handbooks). It is also possible to camp in the country, providing you first obtain permission from the farmer and local police. The season is from May to September, but there are also a large number of winter campgrounds, especially in winter sports areas. Sites are not generally reservable in advance. Rates vary from place to place, but you can expect to pay per car, per person and per tent or camper as well as for electricity and hot showers. In Germany, youth hostels are normally open to card-holders of all ages.

auf dem Campingplatz/at the campground

Gisela, Thomas and Günther are taking Helen camping in the country south of Munich on her last day in Germany.

Thomas: Zelten wir hier unter den zwei großen Bäumen. Gisela, gib mir den Holzhammer und die Heringe fürs Zelt herüber, bitte.

Gisela: (dreamily) Es ist so schön mitten im bayerischen Wald. Endlich kann man die frische Luft atmen—**und was für ein herrlicher Tag!** Es sind keine Wolken am Himmel. Sag mal, Thomas, **hast du die Wettervorhersage heute morgen gehört?**

Thomas: Nein, aber es steht in der Zeitung, daß es den ganzen Tag sonnig wird.

Günther: (gloomily) Heute nacht wird es sicherlich kalt. Auf dem Boden ohne Zeltbetten erfriert man, ja.

Thomas: **Wir können hier im kleinen Campingladen Luftmatratzen mieten.**

Gisela: Ja, und wir brauchen auch eine Landkarte mit Wanderwegen.

Günther: (brightening): Komm, Helen, schauen wir uns den See an. Hast du deinen Badeanzug mitgebracht?

Thomas: (rather upset) Erst steigen wir den Hügel hinauf. Von oben hat man eine großartige Aussicht; und man kann die fernen Berge mit ihren schneebedeckten Gipfeln noch sehen.

Gisela: Ja, ja, und das kleine Kloster da unten . . .

Thomas: Und das Schloß, das Ludwig II gebaut hat . . .

Helen: (laughing) Moment mal—ich muß eine Kassette in meinen Fotoapparat einlegen!

Going camping

Zelten wir hier unter den zwei großen Bäumen.	Let's camp here under the 2 tall trees.
Gib mir den Holzhammer und die Heringe fürs Zelt (herüber).	Pass me the mallet and the tent stakes.
mitten im Wald	in the middle of the woods
Auf dem Boden ohne Zeltbetten erfriert man.	We'll freeze to death on the ground without cots.
Wir können Luftmatratzen mieten.	We can rent air mattresses.
im kleinen Campingladen	in the little camping supply store
eine Landkarte mit Wanderwegen	a map with trails
Darf man hier campen?	Can we camp here?
campen/zelten	camp/camp (pitch a tent)
Es kostet 6,–DM pro Nacht.	It costs 6 marks a night.

der Zeltplatz	site	die Büchse	can
das Zelt	tent	der Dosenöffner	can opener
der Hering	stake	das Taschen- messer	pocket knife
die Zeltstange	tent pole		
der Schlafsack	sleeping bag	die Wasser- flasche	water bottle
der Kocher	stove		
das Camping-Gas	propane gas	der Wasserhahn	tap/water faucet
die Taschen- lampe	flashlight	Ist das Trink- wasser?	Is that drinking water?
der Waschraum	washroom	der Wohnwagen	camper
der Laden	shop	der Anhänger	trailer
der Stromanschluß	electricity	die Jugend- herberge	youth hostel
Streichhölzer	matches		
der Korkenzieher	corkscrew		

ZELTEN/CAMPING VERBOTEN	*NO CAMPING*
KEIN TRINKWASSER	*NOT DRINKING WATER*
TOILETTEN U. DUSCHEN	*TOILETS & SHOWERS*

On vacation (in den Ferien)

Es steht in der Zeitung	It says in the paper
Man kann die frische Luft atmen.	One can breathe the fresh air.
Schauen wir uns den See an.	Let's have a look at the lake.
Steigen wir den Hügel hinauf.	Let's climb up the hill.
eine großartige Aussicht	a magnificent view
die fernen Berge	the distant mountains
mit ihren schneebedeckten Gipfeln	with their snow-covered peaks
das kleine Kloster da unten	the little monastery below
das Schloß, das der König gebaut hat	the castle that the king built

Talking about the weather

(For a list of weather vocabulary, see p. 80.)

Was für ein herrlicher Tag!	What a glorious day!
Was für ein schrecklicher Tag!	What a dreadful day!
Was für ein schönes Wetter!	What lovely weather!
Was für ein furchtbares Wetter!	What terrible weather!
Hast du die Wettervorhersage gehört?	Have you heard the weather forecast?
Wie ist das Wetter?	What's the weather like?
Es sind keine Wolken am Himmel.	There isn't a cloud in the sky.
Es wird sonnig den ganzen Tag.	It will be sunny all day.

Fotografieren (taking pictures)

Ich muß eine Kassette in meinen Fotoapparat einlegen.	I must put a roll of film in my camera.
das Foto, das Bild	photo, picture
der Fotoapparat/die Kamera	camera
Einen Film mit vierundzwanzig Aufnahmen, bitte.	A roll of film with 24 exposures, please.
einen Film entwickeln	to develop a roll of film

Up and down

aufsteigen	to climb up	**bergauf**	uphill
absteigen	to climb down	**bergab**	downhill
hinauf up, upwards, up there		**oben** above, at the top	
hinab down, downwards, down there		**unten** below, beneath, at the foot	

the way it works

Plural nouns after mit, etc.

eine Landkarte **mit** Wanderweg**en**	a map with trails
die Berge, **mit ihren** schneebedeck**ten** Gipfeln	the mountains, with their snow-covered peaks
Zelten wir **unter** den groß**en** Bäumen.	We'll camp under the tall trees.
Note the **n** at the end of the plural noun.	

The castle that Ludwig built

Die Schloß, **das** Ludwig II gebaut hat	The castle that Ludwig II built
Die Abtei, **die** wir gestern besucht haben	The abbey which we visitied yesterday
Der See, **den** Günther und Helen sehen wollen	The lake the Günther and Helen want to see
Die Ruinen, **die** wir besuchen wollen	The ruins that we want to visit

When the word for "that" or "which" is the object of the clause, use **den** for a masculine noun in the singular.

things to do

7.1 You want to camp, but don't have much equipment. Can you ask the camping store clerk for what you need?

1 You'd like to rent a tent and two cots.
2 You need some propane gas for your stove.
3 You'd like to buy some matches and a canteen.
4 You'd like a battery for your flashlight.
5 Ask if there is drinking water from the tap.

7.2

Look at the weather map.
1 What is the weather like in Reykjavik?
2 What is it like in Lisbon?
3 What is it like in Paris and Frankfurt?
4 What kind of weather are they having in northern Scandinavia?
5 What is happening in Sicily?

Deutscher Wetterdienst

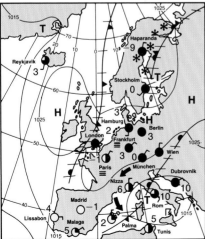

Vorhersagekarte für den 30. Nov.

Zeichenerklärung:

○	wolkenlos
◔	heiter
◑	halb bedeckt
◕	wolkig
●	bedeckt
⌀	Nordwind 10 km/h
⌀	Ostwind 20 km/h
⌀	Südwind 30 km/h
⌀	Westwind 40 km/h

Temperatur in Grad Celsius

≡	Nebel
⁹	Sprühregen
●	Regen
∿	gefrierender Regen
✳	Schnee
▼	Schauer
⌁	Gewitter
▨	Niederschlagsgebiet
▲▲	Warmfront
⌒▲	Okklusion
▲▲▲	Kaltfront am Boden
△△	Kaltfront in der Höhe
⟹	Luftströmung warm
⟹	Luftströmung kalt
H	Hochdruckzentrum
T	Tiefdruckzentrum
h	Sekundär Hoch
t	Sekundär Tief
∼	Isobaren

71

SIGHTSEEING AND EXCURSIONS

▶ ▶ ▶ **Tourist information**   For details on sightseeing tours and excursions,
lists of local events and information about the many carnivals and festivals
held during the tourist season (e.g., beer and music festivals in Germany),
go to the **Fremdenverkehrsbüro** (tourist office). The staff will also assist
you in finding accommodations, checking bus and train times, etc., and
they have many brochures and leaflets, most free of charge. Tourist offices
are located at the main train stations, or in town centers.

eine Stadtrundfahrt/a city tour

Ernst Fischer proposes to take George on a tour of the city of Sunday
afternoon.

Ernst: Heute nachmittag **machen wir eine Stadtrundfahrt**, George.
           Wir werden alle Sehenswürdigkeiten anschauen—die
           Innenstadt, den Viktualienmarkt, das Siegestor, die Brunnen,
           das Schloß Nymphenburg . . .

George: Herrlich! **Ich muß auch einige Geschenke** für meine Frau und
           Jeremy, Helens Bruder in England, **kaufen**. Wo kann ich etwas
           für die Gegend Typisches finden?

Ernst: Fragen wir im Fremdenverkehrsbüro. (looking around as a
           young woman approaches) Aha, darf ich Ihnen Frau Gudrun
           Schultz, eine Mitarbeiterin vom Büro in Frankfurt, vorstellen.
           Frau Schultz ist Sekretärin des Geschäftsführers.

George:	Schön, Sie kennenzulernen.
Ernst:	Na, Gudrun, die Messe ist zu Ende! Sind Sie jetzt auf Urlaub?
Gudrun:	Ja. **Ich möchte gern einen Ausflug ins Gebirge machen**, aber heute abend will ich **München bei Nacht sehen**.
George:	München bei Nacht? Das klingt sehr interessant.
Gudrun:	(to both) Möchten Sie gern mitkommen? Wir können alle drei zusammen gehen.
Ernst:	Leider bin ich heute abend beschäftigt. Wie schade!
George:	(hastily) Danke, ich komme sehr gern.
Gudrun:	(turning to go) Also, bis heute abend— zwanzig Uhr am Karlsplatz.
Ernst:	Tschüß, Gudrun.
George:	Auf Wiedersehen, Frau Schultz. Bis heute abend!

Going on trips and excursions

Machen wir eine Rundfahrt.	Let's go on a tour.
eine Stadtrundfahrt	a tour of the town
Wir werden alle Sehenswürdigkeiten anschauen.	We'll see all the sights.
Besuchen wir . . .	Let's visit . . .
die Innenstadt/die Altstadt	the city center/the old town
den Viktualienmarkt/das Siegestor	the food market/the triumphal arch
die Brunnen/das Schloß Nymphenburg	the fountains/Nymphenburg castle
Ich bin auf Urlaub/geschäftlich hier.	I am here on vacation/on business.
Ich möchte gern einen Ausflug ins Gebirge machen.	I'd love to go on a trip to the mountains.
Ich möchte München bei Nacht sehen.	I'd like to see Munich by night.

Making tourist enquiries

Ich muß einige Geschenke/Souvenirs kaufen.	I must buy some presents/souvenirs.
Wo ist das Reisebüro?	Where is the travel agency?
Wo kann ich etwas für die Gegend Typisches finden?	Where can I find something typical of the region?
Fragen wir im Fremdenverkehrsbüro.	We'll ask at the tourist office.
Wo ist die Informationstelle?	Where is the information booth?
der Verkehrsverein/das Verkehrsamt?	the tourist bureau?
Haben Sie einen Reiseführer?	Do you have a guidebook?

Introducing a colleague

Darf ich Ihnen Frau Schultz vorstellen?	May I introduce Frau Schultz?
eine Mitarbeiterin vom Büro in Frankfurt	a colleague from the Frankfurt office
Schön, Sie kennenzulernen.	Pleased to meet you.
kennenlernen	to get to know
Sie ist Sekretärin des Geschäftsführers.	She's the manager's secretary.
Sie arbeitet in einem Büro.	She works in an office.
Ich bin . . .	I'm a/an . . .
(For a list of jobs and workplaces, see p. 81.)	
Helens Bruder in England	Helen's brother in England
Das klingt interessant.	That sounds interesting.
alle drei zusammen	all three together
Ich bin beschäftigt.	I'm busy.
Tschüß	Goodbye (familiar)

the way it works

Possession

The director's secretary; the secretary of the director.
In German, there is a special way of saying "the" and "s."

die Sekretärin **des** Direktor**s** (m)	the director's secretary
der Chef **der** Fabrik (f)	the head of the factory
der Geschäftsführer **des** Hotel**s** (n)	the manager of the hotel

When talking about people, use an **s** without an apostrophe:

Gisela ist Karl-Heinrich**s** Schwester	Gisela is Karl-Heinrich's sister
Jeremy ist Helen**s** Bruder	Jeremy is Helen's brother

The same endings are also used after **während** (during) and **wegen** (because of), and nouns taking these endings are said to be in the genitive (possessive) case.

things to do

7.3 You go into a **Fremdenverkehrsbüro in Germany.**
1 Ask if they have a guidebook for the town.
2 Ask where you can buy some souvenirs for your family.
3 Ask if there is a tour of the city you can go on.
4 Say you'd like to go on an excursion to the mountains.
5 Ask if there is a travel agency nearby.

7.4 *Was sind sie von Beruf?*
What do these people do for a living?

1 Ich arbeite in einer Schule.
  Ah, Sie sind Lehrer!
2 Ich arbeite in einer Bank.
  . . . .
3 Ich arbeite in einem Büro.

4 Ich arbeite in einem Krankenhaus.
  . . . .
5 Ich arbeite in einer Garage.
  . . . .

1.1 1 Ja, ich bin Herr Lowe. 2 Nein, ich bin Fräulein Leclerc. 3 Nein, ich heiße Tyler. 4 Ja, ich bin Herr Garcia. 5 Nein, ich heiß Brown . . . Ich heiß/Ich bin/Mein Name ist . . .

1.2 1 Guten Tag, Herr Schneider. Wie geht's? 2 Guten Morgen, Frau Schwarz. 3 Guten Abend . . . Sehr erfreut. 4 Guten Tag. Wie geht es Ihnen?

1.3 2 . . . meine Mutter. 3 . . . ist mein Bruder. 4 . . . ist mein Schwester. . . . Das ist Ludwig, mein Mann/Das ist Thomas, mein Sohn/Das ist Gisela, meine Tochter/Das ist Karl-Heinrich, mein Sohn.

1.4 1 Ich möchte ein Einzelzimmer. 2–ein Einzelzimmer mit Fernsehen. 3–ein Doppelzimmer mit Bad. 4–ein Zimmer mit zwei Betten, mit Balkon. 5–ein Einzelzimmer mit Frühstück/Übernachtung mit Frühstück.

1.5 1 Nein, für eine Person. 2 Nein, ich bleibe zwei Nächte. 3 Nein, ich möchte ein Zimmer nach vorn. 4 Es kostet zweihundertfünfzig DM pro Tag. zweihundertfünfzig DM pro Tag.

1.6 2 Er kommt aus England. 3 Er kommt aus der Schweiz. 4 Er kommt aus Österreich. 5 Sie kommt aus Amerika.

2.1 2 Spiegeleier mit Speck, Toast mit Honig, schwarzen Kaffee. 3 Schwarz-brot, Schinken, Tee mit Zitrone. 4 Orangensaft, ein Stück Toast mit Apfelsinenmarmelade, eine Tasse Tee mit Milch. 5 Brot, Käse, heiße Schokolade.

2.2 DM 9,50

2.3 1 Aber sie ist zu eng. 2 Aber sie sind zu teuer. 3 Ich habe die Farbe nicht gern. 4 Ich nehme es.

2.4 1 Ich esse lieber ein Schinkenbrot mit Kartoffelchips. 2 Ich esse lieber ein Omelett mit Käse, und Pommes Frites. 3 Ich esse lieber ein deutsches Beefsteak mit Kartoffelsalat. 4 Ich esse lieber eine Currywurst.

2.5 1 Für ihn, ein Glas Altbier. 2 Für sie, ein Glas Weißwein. 3 Für sie, eine Karaffe Rosé. 4 Für ihn, ein Glas Apfelwein. 5 Für sie, ein Glas Tomatensaft. 6 Für ihn, ein Glas Mineralwasser. 7 Für sie, eine Flasche Whisky.

3.1 1 The museum. 2 The bank. 3 The hospital.

3.2 2 Sie gehen am besten zu Fuß. 3 Sie fahren am besten mit dem Bus. 4 Sie fahren am besten mit dem Zug. 5 Sie fahren am besten mit dem Bus/Sie gehen am besten zu Fuß. 6 Sie gehen am besten zu Fuß.

3.3 1 Wann fährt der nächste Zug nach Frankfurt? 2 Von welchem Gleis? 3 Muß ich umsteigen? 4 Wann/Um wieviel Uhr kommt der Zug an? 5 Kann ich einen Sitzplatz reservieren?

4.1 1 (a), 2 (a), 3 (c), 4 (c).

4.2 1 Ich möchte fünfzig Dollar in Deutsche Mark wechseln. 2 Ich möchte einen Reisescheck einlösen. 3 Wie ist der Wechselkurs heute? 4 Kann ich einen Euroscheck einlösen? Mein Paß ist im Hotel, aber ich habe eine Scheckkarte oder eine Kreditkarte.

4.3 1 Postlagernde Sendung. 2 Was kostet ein Brief nach Amerika, bitte? 3 Drei Briefmarken zu siebzig Pfennig, bitte. 4 Ich möchte ein Paket in die Vereinigten Staaten/nach New York schicken. Was macht das, bitte? 5 Ich möchte eine Internationale Postanweisung einlösen. 6 Wieviel kostet eine Postkarte nach Australien?

5.1 1 Dreißig Liter Super, bitte. 2 Kann ich den Reifendruck prüfen, bitte? 3 Bitte prüfen Sie die Batterie. 4 Führen Sie Reparaturen aus?

5.2 1 Ich möchte ein kleines Auto/einen kleinen Wagen mieten. 2 Wieviel kostet es für zwei Tage? 3 Muß ich eine Kautionssumme zahlen? 4 Ich möchte den Wagen in Stuttgart lassen. 5 Ich nehme den blauen Volkswagen. Geben Sie mir bitte den Schlüssel.

5.3 1 Ausfahrt. 2 (b). 3 (b).

5.4 A Nein, hier Helen Jackson/Helen Jackson am Apparat . . . Einen Augenblick, bitte—das tut mir leid, sie ist nicht hier . . . Sie kommt um half sechs wieder zurück, glaube ich . . . Auf

Wiederhören. B Ich möchte Thomas sprechen, bitte . . . Hier Helen Jackson/ Helen Jackson am Apparat . . . Nein, ich rufe wieder an . . . Auf Wiederhören.

5.5 1 Er hat Magenschmerzen. 2 Sie hat Schmerzen im Fuß. 3 Er hat Kopfschmerzen. 4 Sie hat im Rücken Schmerzen/Der Rücken tut ihr weh. 5 Er hat Zahnschmerzen.

5.6 1 (a). 2 (a) Wo ist die nächste Apotheke? (b) Ich habe mich übergeben. Haben Sie etwas gegen Magenschmerzen? (c) Ich habe mir den Finger verbrannt und ich möchte ein Schmerzmittel. Brauche ich ein Rezept? (d) Wie oft soll ich die Tabletten einnehmen? (e) Ich möchte auch Antiseptikum and Watte.

5.7 1 (a), 2 (c), 3 (b).

5.8 Sleeping pills.

6.1 1 (c), 2(f), 3(a), 4(b), 5(d), 6(e).

6.2 1 (c), 2 Ski poles.

6.3 1 16 Marks. 2 10 minutes in the solarium. 3 Family, friends and acquaintances.

6.4 1 Recently (newly opened). 2 In the heart of the city. (Opposite the Münchner Hof Hotel in Goethestraße.) 3 Every day from 8 p.m.

6.5 e.g. 2 Sie will ein Konzert hören. 3 Er würde gern ins/zum Kino gehen. 4 Sie will tanzen gehen.

6.6 A 1 Um wieviel Uhr endet das Konzert? 2 Gibt es eine Ermäßigung für Studenten? 3 Ich möchte zwei Plätze im Balkon, nach vorn, bitte.

B 1 Der Eintrittspreis ist drei Mark. 2 Die Öffnungszeiten sind von elf bis achtzehn Uhr. 3 Es ist am Montag geschlossen.

C 1 Um wieviel Uhr beginnt die Vorstellung? 2 Kann ich die Plätze reservieren? 3 Einen Platz im Parkett/ Einmal Parkett, bitte.

7.1 Ich möchte ein Zelt und zwei Zeltbetten mieten. 2 Ich brauche Camping-Gas für meinen Kocher. 3 Ich möchte Streichhölzer und eine Wasserflasche kaufen/Geben Sie mir bitte . . . 4 Ich möchte auch eine Batterie für meine Taschenlampe. 5 Ist das Trinkwasser im Wasserhahn?

7.2 1 Cloudy, 3°. 2 Clear skies, 4°. 3 Paris: fairly cloudy, − 1°; Frankfurt: completely overcast, 3°. 4 Cloudy, with snow. 5 Thunderstorms.

7.3 1 Haben Sie einen Reiseführer von der Stadt? 2 Wo kann ich einige Souvenirs für meine Familie kaufen? 3 Gibt es eine Stadtrundfahrt? 4 Ich möchte einen Ausflug ins Gebirge machen. 5 Gibt es eine Reisebüro in der Nähe?

7.4 2 Ah, Sie sind Bankbeamte/in. 3 Ah, Sie sind Sekretärin/Geschäftsmann/ frau, etc. 4 Ah, Sie sind Arzt/ Krankenschwester. 5 Ah, Sie sind Mechaniker.

English–German topic vocabularies

Months of the year (Die Monate)

January	**Januar**	May	**Mai**	September	**September**
February	**Februar**	June	**Juni**	October	**Oktober**
March	**März**	July	**Juli**	November	**November**
April	**April**	August	**August**	December	**Dezember**

in July	**im Juli**	next week	**nächste Woche**
last month	**im letzten Monat**	last year	**letztes Jahr**
last week	**letzte Woche**	next year	**nächstes Jahr**
next month	**im nächsten Monat**	this year	**dieses Jahr**

The seasons (Die Jahreszeiten)

spring	**der Frühling**	autumn/fall	**der Herbst**
summer	**der Sommer**	winter	**der Winter**

The time (Die Zeit)

day	**der Tag(-e)**	year	**das Jahr(-e)**
month	**der Monat(-e)**	clock	**die Uhr(-en)**
week	**die Woche(-n)**	hour	**die Stunde(-n)**
weekend	**das Wochenende(-n)**	minute	**die Minute(-n)**
		second	**die Sekunde(-n)**

Numbers 1–1000

1	**eins**	6	**sechs**	11	**elf**	16	**sechzehn**
2	**zwei**	7	**sieben**	12	**zwölf**	17	**siebzehn**
3	**drei**	8	**acht**	13	**dreizehn**	18	**achtzehn**
4	**vier**	9	**neun**	14	**vierzehn**	19	**neunzehn**
5	**fünf**	10	**zehn**	15	**fünfzehn**	20	**zwanzig**

21	**einundzwanzig**	29	**neunundzwanzig**	80	**achtzig**
22	**zweiundzwanzig**	30	**dreißig**	90	**neunzig**
23	**dreiundzwanzig**	31	**einunddreißig**	100	**hundert**
24	**vierundzwanzig**	40	**vierzig**	101	**hunderteins**
25	**fünfundzwanzig**	50	**fünfzig**	200	**zweihundert**
26	**sechsundzwanzig**	60	**sechzig**	500	**fünfhundert**
27	**siebenundzwanzig**	70	**siebzig**	1000	**tausend**

Ordinal numbers

the first	**der erste,**	the tenth	**der zehnte**
the second	**der zweite**	the 20th	**der zwanzigste**
the third	**der dritte**	the 21st	**der einundzwanzigste**
the fourth	**der vierte**	the 30th	**der dreißigste**
the fifth	**der fünfte**	the 50th	**der füngzigste**
the sixth	**der sechste**	the 82nd	**der zweiundachtzigste**
the seventh	**der siebente/siebte**	the 100th	**der hundertste**
the eighth	**der achte**	the 1000th	**der tausendste**
the ninth	**der neunte**		

Der wievielte ist heute?   What's the date today?
Heute ist der fünfte Juni.   It's the 5th of June.

Clothes (Die Kleidung)

blouse	die Bluse (-n)	scarf	das Halstuch (¨ er)
blouson	der Blouson	shirt	das Hemd (-en)
boots	die Steifel (pl.)	shoes	die Schuhe (pl.)
bra	der Büstenhalter (-)/BH	skirt	der Rock (¨ e)
briefs	der Schlüpfer (-)	socks	die Socken (pl.)
cardigan	die Wolljacke (-n)	stockings/hose	die Strümpfe (pl.)
coat	der Mantel (¨)	suit (man's)	der Anzug (¨ e)
dress	das Kleid (-er)	sweater	der Pullover (-)
gloves	die Handschuhe (pl.)	sweatshirt	das Sweatshirt (-s)
gym shoes	die Turnschuhe (pl.)	sweatsuit	der Trainingsanzug (¨ e)
hat	der Hut (¨ e)	swimsuit	der Badeanzug (¨ e)
jacket	die Jacke (-n)	T-shirt	das T-shirt (-s)
jeans	die Jeans (pl.)	tie	der Krawatte (-n)
nightgown	das Nachthemd (-en)	tights	die Strumpfhose (-n)
pajamas	der Schlafanzug (¨ e)	underpants	die Unterhose (-n)/der
pants	die Hose (-n)		Slip (-s)
raincoat	der Regenmantel (¨)	windbreaker	der Anorak (-s)

Colors (Die Farben)

black	schwarz	purple	purpur
blue	blau	red	rot
brown	braun	white	weiß
green	grün	yellow	gelb
grey	grau	dark	dunkel
pink	rosa	light	hell

Materials

cotton	Baumwolle	nylon	Nylon
denim	Stoff	silk	Seide
leather	Leder	suede	Wildleder
linen	Leinen	wool	Wolle

At the pharmacy

adhesive bandage	das Heftpflaster	laxative	das Abführmittel
		medicine	die Medizin (-)
antiseptic	die Antiseptikum	painkiller	das Schmerzmittel
bandage	der Verband (¨e)	pill	die Pille (-n)
cotton ball	die Watte	tablet	die Tablette (-n)
cough syrup	der Hustensaft	thermometer	das Thermometer
eye drops	die Augentropfen	throat lozengers	die Halspastillen

Toiletries (Die Toilettenartikel)

aftershave	das Rasierwasser	razor blades	die Rasierklingen
babyfood	die Babynahrung (-)	safety pins	die Sicherheitsnadel
brush	die Bürste (-n)	sanitary napkins	die Damenbinden
comb	der Kamm (¨e)		
contact lens cleaner	der Kontaklinsenreiniger	shampoo	das Haarwaschmittel (-)
		shaving cream	die Rasiercreme
contraceptives	die Verhütungsmittel	soap	die Seife (-n)
deodorant	das Deodorant	suntan lotion	die Sonnenmilch
disposable diapers	die Wegwerf-Windeln	talc	das Körperpuder (-)
		tampons	die Tampons
lotion	die Creme (-s)	tissues	die Papiertücher
perfume	das Parfüm (-e)	toothbrush	die Zahnbürste (-n)
razor	der Rasierapparat (-e)	toothpaste	die Zahnpasta

VOCABULARY

Food

Fish (Der Fisch)

carp	der Karpfen (-)	lobster	der Hummer (-)
cod	der Kabeljau (-e)	mackerel	die Makrele (-n)
crab	der Krebs (-e)	prawns	die Garnelen (pl.)
eel	der Aal (-e)	salmon	der Lachs (-e
flounder	die Scholle (-n)	shrimp	die Krabben (pl.)
haddock	der Schellfisch (-e)	sole	die Seezunge (-n)
halibut	der Heilbutt (-e)	trout	die Forelle (-n)
herring	der Hering (-e)	tuna	der Thunfisch (-e)

Meat (Das Fleisch)

chop	das Kotelett (-s)	well done	durchgebraten
cutlet	das Schnitzel (-)	veal	das Kalbfleisch
kidneys	die Nieren	breaded veal	Wiener Schnitzel
liver	die Leber	cutlet	
steak	das Steak (-s)	lamb	das Hammelfleisch/
beef	das Rindfleisch		der Lamm
braised beef	der Rostbraten	lamb chop	das Lammkotelett
goulash	das Gulasch	roast lamb	der Lammbraten
meat loaf	der Hackbraten	pork	das Schweinefleisch
minced meat	das Hackfleisch	bacon	der Speck
ribs	das Rippensteak	ham	der Schinken
steak	das Filetsteak	knuckle of pork	das Eisbein
rare	blutig	chop	die Rippchen
medium	mittel/medium		

Poultry and game (Das Geflügel und das Wild)

chicken	das Hähnchen (-)/	partridge	das Rebhuhn (¨er)
	das Huhn (¨er)	pheasant	der Fasan (-e)
duck	die Ente (-n)	pigeon	die Taube (-n)
goose	die Gans (¨e)	rabbit	das Kaninchen (-)
hare	der Hase (-n)	turkey	der Truthahn (¨e)

Vegetables (Die Gemüse)

asparagus	der Spargel (-)	onion	die Zwiebel (-n)
bean	die Bohne (-n)	pea	die Erbse (-n)
broccoli	der Braunkohl (-e)	pickled cabbage	das Sauerkraut (¨er)
Brussels sprouts	der Rosenkohl (sing.)	potato	die Kartoffel (-n)
cabbage	der Kohl (-e)	boiled	Salzkartoffeln
carrot	die Karotte (-n)	boiled in skins	Pellkartoffeln
cauliflower	der Blumenkohl (-e)	fried	Bratkartoffeln
celery	die Sellerie	mashed	der Kartoffelbrei
cucumber	die Salatgurke (-n)	radishes	die Radieschen (pl.)
dumplings	die Klöße/die Knödel (pl.)	red cabbage	das Blaukraut/
eggplant	die Aubergine		der Rotkohl
garlic	der Knoblauch	spätzle	die Spätzle (pl.)
gherkin	die Essiggurke (-n)	spinach	der Spinat (-e)
leek	der Lauch (-e)	sweetcorn	der Mais
lettuce	der Kopfsalat (-e)	tomato	die Tomate (-n)
mushroom	der Pilz (-e)	turnip	der Kohlrabi
noodles	die Nudeln (pl.)	zucchini	die Zucchetti (pl.)

VOCABULARY

Fruit (Das Obst)

apple	der Apfel (die Äpfel)
apricot	die Aprikose (-n)
banana	die Banane (-n)
blackberry	die Brombeere (-n)
cherry	die Kirsche (-n)
grapefruit	die Pampelmuse (-n)
grape	die Traube (-n)
lemon	die Zitrone (-n)
orange	die Apfelsine (-n)
peach	der Pfirsich (-e)
pear	die Birne (-n)
pineapple	die Ananas (-)
plum	die Pflaume (-n)
raspberry	die Himbeere (-n)
red/	Rote/Schwarze
blackcurrents	Johannisbeeren (pl.)
rhubarb	der Rhabarber
strawberry	die Erdbeere (-n)

Weather (Das Wetter)

clear	heiter
cloudless	wolkenlos
cloudy	wolkig
drizzle	der Sprühregen
fog	der Nebel
hail	der Hagel
ice	das Eis
lightning	der Blitz (-e)
rain	der Regen
rainfall	der Niederschlag
shower	der Schauer (-)
snow	der Schnee
storm	der Sturm (¨e)
thunder	der Donner (-)
thunderstorm	das Gewitter (-)

Car parts

accelator	das Gaspedal	ignition	die Zündung
alternator	der Wechselstromzeug	license plate	das Nummernschild
brakes	die Bremsen	radiator	der Kühler
bulb	die Glühbirne	seat belt	der Sicherheitsgurt (-e)
bumper	die Stoßstange	sparkplugs	die Zündkerzen
carburetor	der Vergaser	starter	der Anlasser
clutch	die Kupplung	steering wheel	das Lenkrad
engine	der Motor	tires	die Reifen
exhaust	der Auspuff	trunk	der Kofferraum
fan-belt	der Keilriemen	turn signals	die Blinker
fuses	die Sicherungen	wheel	das Rad (¨er)
gear box	das Getriebe	windshield	die Windschutz-
headlights	die Scheinwerfer		scheibe
horn	die Hupe	wipers	die Scheibenwischer

Sport (Der Sport)

archery	das Bogenschießen	judo	das Judo
badminton	der Federball	racing	das Autorennen
basketball	der Basketball	rollerskating	das Rollschuhlaufen
billiards/pool	das Billardspiel	rugby	das Rugby
chess	das Schachspielen	sailing	das Segeln
climbing	das Bergsteigen	shooting	das Schießen
cycling	das Radfahren	skating	das Schlittschuhlaufen
fishing	das Angeln	skiiing	das Skifahren
golf	das Golf	soccer	der Fußball
handball	der Handball	sunbathing	das Baden
hang-gliding	das Drachenfliegen	swimming	das Schwimmen
hiking, walking	das Wandern	tennis	das Tennis
hockey	das Hockey	volleyball	der Volleyball
horse-back riding	das Reiten	water skiing	das Wasserskifahren
horce racing	das Pferderennen	wind surfing	das Windsurfen
hunting	die Jagd	winter sports	der Wintersport
jogging	der Jogging	yoga	der Yoga

VOCABULARY

Parts of the body

arm	der Arm (-e)	hand	die Hand (¨e)
back	der Rücken (-)	head	der Kopf (¨e)
body	der Körper (-)	heart	der Herz (-en)
blood	das Blut	knee	das Knie (-n)
breast	die Brust (¨e)	lip	die Lippe (-n)
chest	der Brustkorb (¨er)	leg	das Bein (-e)
ear	das Ohr (-en)	mouth	der Mund (¨er)
elbow	der Ellbogen (-)	neck	der Hals (¨e)
eye	das Auge (-n)	nose	die Nase (-n)
face	das Gesicht (-er)	shoulder	die Schulter (-n)
finger	der Finger (-)	stomach	der Magen (-)
foot	der Fuß (Füße)	toe	die Zehe (-n)
hair	das Haar (-e)	tongue	die Zunge (-n)

Jobs (Die Arbeit)

accountant/bank clerk	Buchhalter/Bankbeamte, -beamtin
businessman, businesswoman	Geschäftsmann, Geschäftsfrau
chef	Küchenchef, -chefin
computer programer	Computer-Programmierer, -erin
director/doctor	Direktor/Arzt
engineer	Ingenieur
factory worker	Fabrikarbeiter/ -erin
fashion designer	Mode-Designer, -erin
head of a firm/company	Chef, Chefin einer Firma/Gesellschaft
housewife/journalist	Hausfrau/Journalist, -istin
lab assistant/lawyer	Laborant, -antin/Rechtsanwalt
lecturer/manager	Dozent, -entin/Geschäftsführer
mechanic/nurse	Mechaniker/Krankenschwester
painter	Maler
salesclerk	Verkäufer, -erin
(sales) representative	Handelsvertreter, -erin
student/teacher	Student, -entin/Lehrer, -erin
technician/writer	Techniker/Schriftsteller, -erin

Workplaces

I work in a/an . . .	Ich arbeite in einem		. . . in einer
		bank	Bank
hospital	Krankenhaus	college	Hochschule
hotel	Hotel	factory	Fabrik
laboratory	Laboratorium	garage	Garage
office	Büro	school	Schule
shop	Laden	university	Universität
studio	Atelier	workshop	Werkstatt

Leisure and entertainment

art gallery	die Kunstgalerie (-n)	monument	das Denkmal (¨e)
ballet	das Ballet (-e)	movies	das Kino (-s)
casino	das Kasino (-s)	museum	das Museum (-een)
cathedral	der Dom (-e)	nightclub	der Nachtclub (-s)
concert	das Konzert (-e)	opera	die Oper (-n)
discotheque	die Diskothek (-s)	play	das Theaterstück (-e)
film	der Film (-e)	theater	das Theater (-)

VOCABULARY

German–English

Plurals of nouns are given in parentheses where appropriate, e.g., **der Anzug** (¨e)—**die Anzüge**.

ab from
Abend *m.* (-e) evening, **am-** in the evening; **guten-** good evening; **abends** in the evening; **-essen** *n.* dinner, supper
aber but
abfahren leave, depart
Abfahrt *f.* (-en) departure
absteigen climb down
Abtei *f.* (-en) abbey
Abteil *n.* (-en) compartment
Adresse *f.* (-n) address
all/aller/alles all, every, everything
allergisch allergic
als when, than
also so, then, well then
alt old; **Altbier** *n.* bitter ale; **Altstadt** *f.* (¨e) old town
am at the
Amerika *n.* America
Amerikaner *m.* (-)/**erin** *f.* (-innen) American (person)
amerikanisch American
Ampel *f.* (-n) traffic lights
an (+ *acc./dat.*) at, to on
anfangen begin
Angeln *n.* fishing
Angelrute *f.* (-n) fishing rod
angenehm pleasant(ly)
Angestellte(r) *f. m.* (-n, -en) employee
ängstlich anxious
ankommen arrive; **es kommt darauf an** that depends
Ankunft *f.* (¨e) arrival
Anorak *m.* (-s) windbreaker
anprobieren try on
anrufen phone
anschauen look at
Anschlagbrett *n.* (-er) notice board
ansehen look at
anspringen start (car)
antworten reply
Anzug *m.* (¨e) suit (man's)
Apfel *m.* (¨) apple; **-wein** *m.* (-e) cider
Apfelsine *f.* (-n) orange
Apfelsinenmarmelade *f.* (-n) orange marmalade

Apotheke *f.* (-n) pharmacy; **Apotheker** *m.* (-) pharmacist
Apparat *m.* (-e) camera, telephone; **am-** on the phone
Appetit *m.* appetite; **guten-!** bon appétit!
Arbeit *f.* (-en) work; **arbeiten** work; **arbeitslos** unemployed
ärgerlich upset, angry
arm poor
Arm *m.* (-e) arm
Arzt *m.* (¨e) doctor
atmen breathe
auch too, also
auf (+ *acc./dat.*) on, in, at; **- Wiedersehen!** goodbye!
aufgeben send (telegram)
Aufnahme *f.* (-n) exposure (film)
aufpassen; paß auf! look out!
aufsteigen climb (up)
Aufzug *m.* (¨e) elevator
Auge *n.* (-n) eye
Augenblick *m.* (-e) moment
aus (+ *acc./dat.*) from, out of
Ausfahrt *f.* (-en) exit
Ausflug *m.* (¨e) excursion/trip; **einen- machen** go on an excursion/trip
ausführen carry out
ausfüllen fill in, up
ausgehen stall (engine)
ausgezeichnet excellent
Auskunft *f.* (¨e) information
Ausland *n.* abroad
ausrichten: kann ich etwas—? can I take a message?
ausruhen, sich rest
Ausrüstung *f.* (-en) equipment
aussehen look, seem
ausstehen, nicht- loathe
außer (+ *dat.*) besides
Aussicht *f.* (-en) view
Ausstellung *f.* (-en) exhibition/ convention; **-shalle** *f.* (-n) exhibition/ convention center
Auto *n.* (-s) car (-**bahn** *f.* (-en) highway; **-vermietung** *f.* (-en) car rental office/service
Automat *m.* (-en) vending machine

VOCABULARY

Bäckerei *f.* (-e) bakery
Bad *n.* (-er) bath; -**eanzug** *m.* (¨e) bathing suit; -**ezimmer** *n.* (-) bathroom
baden bathe
Bahnbeamte(r)/in *f. m.* (-, innen) railroad employee
Bahnhof *m.* (¨e) station
Bahnsteig *m.* (-e) platform
bald soon; **bis** - see you later
Ball *m.* (¨e) ball
Ballet *n.* (-e) ballet
Balkon *m.* (-e) balcony
Banane *f.* (-n) banana
Bank *f.* (-en) bank; -**beamte(r)/in** *m. f.* (-, innen) bank teller
Bar *f.* (-s) bar
Bargeld *n.* cash
Batterie *f* (-e) battery
bauen build
Bauernhof *m.* (¨e) farm
Baum *m.* (¨e) tree
Bayern *n.* Bavaria; **bayerisch** Bavarian
bedeckt overcast
Bedienung *f.* (-en) service
beginnen begin
bei *(+ dat.)* near, at, at the house of
Bein *n.* (-e) leg
Beispiel, zum - (z.B.) for example
Bekannte(r) *m. f.* acquaintance
bekommen get, receive
Benzin *n.* gas
beraten advise
bereit ready
bergab downhill; **bergauf** uphill
Berg *m.* (-e) mountain, hill; -**steigen** *n.* climbing
Beruf *m.* (-e) job, profession; **von** - by profession
beruhigen calm
berühmt famous
beschäftigt busy
besetzt occupied
besonders especially
Bestätigung *f.* (-e) confirmation
bestellen order
besten, am - best
bestimmt right, certain
Besuch *m.* (-e) visit
besuchen visit
Bett *n.* (-en) bed
bewaldet wooded
bewegen move

bezahlen pay
Bier *n.* (-) beer; -**keller** *m.* (-) pub; -**stube** *f.* (-n) pub
Bild *n.* (-er) picture, photo
billig cheap
bin; *see* **sein**
Birne *f.* (-n) pear
bißchen: ein - a little, bit
bitte please; -? pardon?; -**schön!** don't mention it!
blau blue
bleiben stay, remain
blöd stupid
Bluse *f.* (-n) blouse
Blut *n.* blood; **blutig** rare (steak)
Boden *m.* (¨) ground, floor
Bogenschießen *n.* archery
Bohne *f.* (-n) bean
Boot *n.* (-e) boat
Botschaft *f.* (-en) embassy
Bratwurststand *m.* (¨e) sausage stand
brauchen need
braun brown
Bremse *f.* (-n) brake
Brief *m.* (-e) letter; -**kasten** *m.* (¨) mailbox; -**marke** *f.* (-n) stamp; -**tasche** *f.* (-n) wallet
Brille *f.* (-n) glasses
bringen bring
Broschüre *f.* (-n) brochure
Brot *n.* (-e) bread, loaf
Brötchen *n.* (-) roll
Brücke *f.* (-n) bridge
Bruder *m.* (¨) brother
Brunnen *m.* (-) fountain, well
Buch *n.* (¨e) book
Büchse *f.* (-n) can
Bucht *f.* (-en) bay
Burg *f.* (-en) fortress, castle
Bus *m.* (-se) bus; -**haltestelle** *f.* (-n) bus stop

Café *n.* (-s) café
campen camp; **Campingladen** *m.* (¨)camping supply store
Chef/Chefin *m. f.* (-s, innen) boss, chief
Chor *m.* (¨e) choir

da there, then; -**drüben** over there
Dach *n.* (¨er) roof
Dame *f.* (-n) lady; **Damen** ladies (toilets)
Dank, vielen - many thanks; **danke schön** thank you very much

83

VOCABULARY

danken thank
dann then
darf *see* dürfen
das the, that; -ist that is
daß that
Datum *n.* (Daten) date
dauern last
denken think
Denkmal *n.* (¨e) monument
den the
denn for, because
der the
deutsch German; Deutschland *n.*
   Germany; Deutschmark *f.* (-) mark
dich *(acc.)* you (fam.)
die the
dieser/e/es this, that
dir *(dat.)* (to) you (fam.)
Direktor *m.* (-en) manager
Dirigent *m.* (-en) conductor
doch yes (after neg.)
Dom *m.* (e) cathedral
Doppelzimmer *n.* (-) double room
Dorf *n.* (¨er) village
dort there
Dose *f.* (-n) can; -nöffner *m.* (-) can
   opener
Dragee *n.* (-s) pill
Droge *f.* (-n) drug; Drogerie *f.* (-n)
   drugstore
du you (fam.)
dunkel dark
D-Zug (Durchgangszug) *m.* (¨e)
   express train
durch *(+ acc.)* through; -gebraten well
   done (steak)
dürfen may, be allowed to
Durst *m.* thirst; -haben be thirsty
Dusche *f.* (-n) shower
Dutzend *n.* (-e) dozen
eben even, just
Ecke *f.* (-n) corner; in der- in the corner
Ei *n.* (-er) egg
ein/eine/einen/eins a,
   one;Einbahnstraße *f.* one-way street
einfach one-way ticket
Einfahrt *f.* (-en) entrance (highway)
Eingang *m.* (¨e) entrance
einige some
Einkauf *m.* (¨e) purchase; Einkäufe
   machen go shopping
einlösen cash (check, etc.)
einmal once

einlegen put in, insert
einsteigen get in (train, etc.)
eintragen, sich register
Eintritt *m.* entrance, entry, -skarte *f.* (-n)
   admission ticket; -spreis *m.* (-e)
   admission fee
Einzelfahrkarte *f.* (-n) single ticket
Einzelzimmer *n.* (-) single room
Eis *n.* ice, ice cream; -bahn *f.* (-en)
   skating rink; -becher *m.* ice cream
   sundae; -sporthalle *f.* (-n) ice rink
Eisbein *n.* leg of pork
Eltern *pl.* parents
Empfang *m.* (¨e) reception; -sdame *f.*
   (-n) receptionist
empfehlen recommend
Ende: zu - at an end, finished
endlich at last, finally
eng tight, narrow
England *n.* England
Engländer/erin *m. f.* (-, innen)
   Englishman/woman
englisch English
Ente *f.* (-n) duck
entfernt far
entlang *(+ acc.)* along
entschuldigen, sich excuse oneself;
   -Sie excuse me
entwickeln develop (film)
er he
Erbsen *pl.* peas
Erdgeschoß: im - on the ground floor
erfrieren freeze to death
erfreut pleased, glad
Ermäßigung *f.* (-en) reduction, discount
ernst serious
erst first; -mal firstly
Erwachsene *pl.* adults
es it
essen eat; Essen n. meal, eating
Essig *m.* vinegar
etwas something, anything
Euroscheck *m.* (-s) Eurocheck

Fabrik *f.* (-en) factory
fahren go, drive, travel; Fahrer *m.* (-)
   driver
Fahrkarte, Fahrschein *f. m.* (-n, -e)
   ticket
Fahrrad *n.* (¨er) bicycle
Fahrt *f.* (-en) trip; gute -! have a nice
   trip!
Familie *f.* (-n) family

VOCABULARY

Farbe *f.* **(-n)** color
Fenster *n.* **(-n)** window
Ferien *pl.* vacations; **in den** - on vacation
fern distant
Fernsehen *n.* TV
Fernsprecher *m.* **(-)** telephone booth
fertig ready, finished
Fest *n.* **(-e)** festival
Feuer *n.* **(-)** fire; **-wache** *f.* fire station
Fieber *n.* fever
finden find
Finger *m.* **(-)** finger
Firma *m.* **(-en)** firm
Fisch *m.* **(-e)**; fish; **-gericht** *n.* **(-e)** fish dish; **-handlung** *f.* **(-en)** fish market
Flasche *f.* **(-n)** bottle
Fleisch *n.* meat; **(-gerei** *f.* **(en)** butcher shop; **-speise** *f.* **(-n)** meat dish
fliegen fly
Flug *m.* **(¨e)** flight; **-hafen** *m.* **(¨)** airport; **-schein** *m.* **(-e)** airline ticket; **-zeug** *n.* **(-e)** airplane
Fluß *m.* **(¨e)** river
fördern promote, encourage
Forelle *f.* **(-n)** trout
Formular *n.* **(-e)** form
Foto *n.* **(-s)** photo; **fotografieren** take a picture
fragen ask
französisch French
Frau *f.* **(-en)** woman, wife, Mrs.
Fräulein *n.* **(-)** young lady, Miss; waitress
frei free; **Freibad** *n.* **(¨er)** outdoor pool
Fremdenverkehrsbüro *n.* **(-s)** tourist information office
freut: es - mich I like it
Freund *m.* **(-e)/Freundin** *f.* **(innen)** friend; **freundlich** friendly
frieren freeze
frisch fresh
Fruchtsaft *m.* **(¨e)** fruit juice
Frühstück *n.* **(-e)** breakfast; **frühstücken** have breakfast
fühlen, sich feel
Führerschein *m.* **(-e)** driver's license
Fundamt *n.* **(¨er)/Fundbüro** *n.* **(-s)** lost and found
furchtbar dreadful
Fuß *m.* **(¨e)** foot; **zu-,** on foot
Fußball *m.* **(¨e)** soccer; **-spiel** *n.* **(-e)** soccer game; **-platz** *m.* **(¨e)** soccer field
Fußgänger *m.* **(-)** pedestrian

Gabel *f.* **(-n)** fork
ganz quite, whole; **den -en Tag** all day
Garderobe *f.* **(-n)** cloakroom
Garten *m.* **(¨)** garden
Gast *m.* **(¨e)** guest; **-familie** *f.* **(-n)** host family
gebacken baked
Gebäude *n.* **(-)** building
geben give; **es gibt** there is/are
Gebirge *n.* **(-)** mountains
gebissen bitten
gebrochen broken
Gebühren *pl.* charges
Gefahr *f.* **(-en)** danger
gefallen please, like; **es gefällt mir** I like it
Gedeck *n.* **(-e)** special (at a restaurant)
gegen *(+ acc.)* about, against, to(wards), for, **-über** *(+ dat.)* opposite
Gegend *f.* **(-en)** district
gehen go, walk; **wie geht's** how are you? **es geht mir gut** I'm fine
gekocht boiled
gelb yellow
Geld *n.* **(-er)** money; **-schein** *m.* **(-e)** bill (currency); **-strafe** *f.* **(-n)** fine
gemischt mixed
Gemüse *n.* **(-)** vegetable
gemütlich nice, cozy
genau exact(ly)
Gepäck *n.* luggage
gerade straight; **-aus** straight ahead
gern(e) willingly **-haben** to like
Geschäft *n.* **(-e)** store, business; **-smann/frau** *m. f.* **(¨er, -en)** businessman/woman, **-sführer** *m* **(-)** manager; **-sreise** *f* **(-n)** business trip; **-sviertel** *n.* **(-)** business district
geschäftlich on business
Geschenk *n.* **(-e)** present, gift
geschlossen closed
geschwollen swollen
Gesellschaft *f.* **(-en)** company
Gesicht *n.* **(-er)** face
gestern yesterday
gestochen stung
gestohlen stolen
gesund healthy, well; **Gesundheit** *f.* **(-en)** health
Glas *n.* **¨er)** glass
glauben think, believe; **ich glaube schon** I think so
gleich immediate(ly); **mir ist das -** it's all the same to me

VOCABULARY

Gleis *n.* (-e) track
Golf *n.* golf; **-platz** *m.* ("e) golf course
grau grey
Grenze *f.* (-n) border
groß big, large; **-artig** magnificent
grün green
gucken look; **guck mal!** look!
gut good, well

Haar *n.* (-e) hair; **-waschmittel** *n.* (-) shampoo
haben have
Hafen *m.* (") harbor, port
Hähnchen *n.* (-) chicken
halb half; **Halbpension** *f.* half board
Hallenbad *n.* ("er) indoor pool
Hals *m.* ("e) neck
halten keep, hold
Haltestelle *f.* (-n) bus stop
Hammelfleisch *n.* lamb (meat)
Hand *f.* ("e) hand; **-tuch** *n.*)-e) towel; **-schuh** *m.* (-e) glove; **-tasche** *f.* (-n) handbag
hat: *see* **haben**
hätte: ich - gern I'd like
Hauptbahnhof *m.* ("e) main train station
Haus *n.* (er) house; **nach -e** home(wards); **zu -e** at home
heiß hot
heißen be called
heiter clear (sky)
hell light
helfen help
Hemd *n.* (-en) shirt
Hering *m.* (-e) tent stake
Herr *m.* (-en) gentleman, man, Mr.; **-en** gents (toilets); **-Ober!** waiter!
herrlich lovely, splendid
herüber over (here)
Herz *n.* (-en) heart
heute today; **-abend** this evening
heutzutage nowadays
hier here
Hilfe *f.* help; **Erste -** first aid
Himmel *m.* (-) heaven
hin: -und zurück round trip
hinaufsteigen climb up
hinfallen fall down
hinten: nach - at the back, behind
hinter (+ *acc./dat.*) behind; **-lassen** leave behind
hoch high
hoffen hope
holen fetch, bring

Holzhammer *m.* (") mallet
homöopathisch homeopathic
Honig *m.* honey
hören hear
Hose *f.* (-n) trousers
Hotel *n.* (s) hotel
Huhn *n.* ("er) chicken
hundert hundred
Hunger *m.* hunger; **-haben** be hungry
Hupe *f.* (-en) horn
Husten *m.* (-) cough
Hut *m.* ("e) hat
ich I
ihn *(acc.)* him
ihnen *(dat.)* them, to them
Ihnen *(dat.)* you, to you
ihr *(dat.)* her, to her; **-(adj.)** her, their
Ihr *(adj.)* your
im (in + dem) in the
immer always
in (+ *acc./dat.*) in, into, to, at
inbegriffen included
Informationstelle *f.* (-n) information desk
Ingenieur *m.* (-e) engineer
Insel *f.* (-n) island
interessant interesting; **intessieren, sich (für)** be interested (in)
ist: see **sein**

ja yes
Jacke *f.* (-n) jacket, coat
Jahr *n.* (-e) year; **-eszeit** *f.* (-en) season; **jährlich** annual
jeder/e/es every, each
jedermann everyone
jetzt now
Jugendherberge *f.* (-n) Youth Hostel
jung young
Junge *m.* (-n) boy

Kaffee *m.* (-s) coffee
kalt cold
Kalbfleisch *n.* veal
Kamm *m.* ("er) comb
Kännchen *n.* (-) small pot
kann: see **können**
Kapelle *f.* (-n) band, chapel
kaputt broken
Karotte *f.* (-n) carrot
Karte *f.* (-n) ticket, card, menu
Kartoffel *f.* (-n) potato; **-chips** *pl.* potato chips
Käse *m.* (-) cheese; **-kuchen** *m.* (-) cheesecake

Kasse f. (-n) cashier, check-out
Kassette f. (-n) cassette, cartridge;
  -nrecorder cassette recorder
kaufen buy; **Kaufhaus** n. (¨er)
  department store
kaum scarcely
Kautionssumme f. (-n) deposit
kein/keine/keines no, not any
Keks m. (-e) cookie
Kellner/in m. f. (-, innen) waiter,
  waitress
kennen know; **-lernen** get to know, meet
Kind n. (-er) child
Kino n. (-s) movie theater
Kirche f. (-n) church
Kirsche f. (-n) cherry
Klasse f. (-n) class
Kleid n. (-er) dress
Kleidung f. clothes
klein little, small
Klima n. (-s) climate
klingen sound
Klinik f. (-en) clinic
Kloster n. (¨) monastery, convent
Knöchel m. (-) ankel
Kocher m. (-) stove
Koffer m. (-) bag, suitcase
Knödel m. (-) dumpling
Kohl m. (-) cabbage
Köln n. Cologne
kommen come
Komödie f. (-n) comedy
Konditorei f. (-en) cake shop, café
Konfitüre f. (-n) jam
können can, be able
Konsulat n. (-e) consulate
Konto n. (-ten) account (bank); **-karte** f.
  (-n) bank card
Konzert n. (-e) concert; **-halle** f. (-n)
  concert hall
Kopf m. (¨e) head; **-salat** m. (-) lettuce
Korkenzieher m. (-) corkscrew
Körper m. (-) body; **-puder** m. (-) talc
kosten cost
krank ill; **Krankenhaus** n. (¨er) hospital;
  Krankenschwester f. (-) nurse
Krawatte f. (-n) tie
Kreditkarte f. (-n) credit card
Kreisverkehr m. roundabout
Kreuzung f. (-en) crossing, intersection
Kuchen m. (-) cake, pie
kühl cool
Kunde m. (-n) customer
Kunst f. (¨e) art; **-galerie** f. (-n) art gallery

Künstler m. (-) artist
kurz short; **Kürz-film** m. (-e) short film
Kusine f. (-n) (female) cousin

Land n. (¨er) country; **-karte** f. (-n) map;
  -schaft f. scenery, countryside
lang long; **wie lange?** how long?
langsam slow(ly)
langweilig boring
lassen let, leave
Lastkraftwagen m. (-) truck
laufen run, show (film)
leben live; **Diät-** be on a diet
Lebensmittelgeschäft n. (-) grocery
  store
Leber f. liver; **-wurst** (¨e) liver sausage
leer empty
legen put, place
Lehrer m. (-) teacher
leicht light
leid: das tut mir- I'm sorry; **leider**
  unfortunately
leiden bear, stand
leihen rent
lernen learn
lesen read
letzt last; **-es Jahr** last year; **-e Woche**
  last week
Leute pl. people
lieb dear; **Liebchen** darling
lieber: ich habe - I prefer
liegen lie, be situated
Lift m. (-e) elevator, (ski) lift; **-paß** m. (¨e)
  lift ticket
Limonade f. soda
Linie f. (-n) line, route
link left; **-s** on the left
Liste f. (-n) list
los: was ist los? what's the matter?
Londoner/in m. f. (-, innen) Londoner
Luft f. (¨e) air
Luftmatratze f. (n) air matress
Lust: ich habe - I'd like to

machen make, do; **was macht das?**
  what does that come to?
Mädchen n. (-) girl
mag: see mögen
Magen m. (¨) stomach; **-schmerzen** pl.
  stomachache
Mahlzeit f. (-en) meal
Mal n. (-e) time
mal just, only
Maler m. (-) painter, artist

VOCABULARY

man one, they, etc.
Mann *m.* (¨er) man
Mantel *m.* (¨) coat
Mark *f.* (-) Mark (curr.)
markiert marked
Markt *m.* (¨e) market
Marmelade *f.* (-n) jam
Maß *n.* (-e) measurement
Mauer *f.* (-n) wall
Mechaniker *m.* (-) mechanic
Medikament *n* (-e) medicine
Medizin *f.* (-) medicine
Meer *n.* (-e) sea
Mehl *n.* (-e) flour
mehr more
Mehrwertsteuer *f.* sales tax
mein/meine/meines my
Menü *n.* (-s) set menu
Messe *f.* (-n) convention, fair; -gelände *n.* fair ground
Messer *n.* (-) knife
Metzgerei *f.* (-en) butcher shop
mich *(acc.)* me
mieten rent
mild mild, calm
Mineralwasser *n.* (-) mineral water
mir *(dat.)* me, to me
mit *(+ dat.)* with; -bringen bring with; -gebracht brought with; -kommen come with, accompany
Mitarbeiter/in *m. f.* (-, innen) colleague
Mittag *m.* midday; -essen *n.* (-) lunch; -spause *f.* (-n) lunch break
Mittel *n.* (-) remedy, means
mittel medium
mitten in in the middle of
Mitternacht *f.* midnight
möchte: ich - I would like
mögen may, like
möglich possible
Moment *m.* (-e) moment; einen -/- mal just a moment
Monat *m.* (-e) month
Morgen *m.* (-) morning; guten - good morning; morgens in the morning
morgen tomorrow; -früh tomorrow morning
Motor *m.* (-en) engine, motor
Motorrad *n.* (¨er) motorcycle
müde tired
München Munich; Münchner *(adj.)* Munich
Mund *m.* (-e) mouth
Museum *n.* (-en) museum

müssen must, have to; ich muß I must
Mutter *f.* (¨) mother; Mutti *f.* Mom(my)
nach *(+ dat.)* after, to
Nachmittag *m.* (-e) afternoon
    nachmittags in the afternoon
Nachtricht *f.* (-en) message
Nachtisch *m.* (-e) dessert
nächst next
Nacht *f.* (¨e) night
nah near; in der Nähe in the vicinity, nearby
Name *m.* (-n) name
Nase *f.* (-n) nose
naß wet
natürlich naturally, of course
neben *(+ acc./dat.)* near, beside
nehmen take
nein no
nett nice
neu new
nicht not; -s nothing
Nieren *pl.* kidneys
nimmt: *see* nehmen
noch yet, again, still; -einmal another one; -mal again
Nord, Norden *m.* north
Normal *n.* regular (gas)
Notausgang *m.* (¨e) emergency exit
Notdienst *m.* (-e) emergency service
Notfall *m.* (¨e) emergency; im- in an emergency
Nummer *f.* (-n) number
nun now
nur only

oben on top
Ober: Herr-! waiter!
Obst *n.* fruit; -kuchen *m.* (-) fruit pie; -torte *f.* (-n) fruit torte
oder or
offen open; öffnen *(verb)* open;
    Öffnungszeiten *pl.* business hours
ohne *(+ acc.)* without
Ohr *n.* (-en) ear
Öl *n.* oil
Oper *f.* (-n) opera
Orangensaft *m.* (¨e) orange juice
Orchester *n.* (-) orchestra
Ordnung *f.* (-en) order; in- in order
Ost, Osten *m* east

Paar *n.* (-e) pair; ein paar a few
Packung *f.* (-en) package, bag
Paket *n.* (-e) packet, parcel

VOCABULARY

Panne f. (-n) breakdown
Papier n. (-e) paper
Parfüm n. (-e) perfume
Park m. (-s) park
Parkett n. orchestra seats
Parkplatz f. ("e) parking lot;
    Parkscheibe f. (-n) parking sticker;
    Parkuhr f. (-en) parking meter
Party f. party
Paß m. ("e) passport
Passant m. (-en) passer-by
passen fit; es paßt ihnen it fits you
passieren to happen, pass; passiert
    happened
Person f. (-en) person
Pfeffer n. pepper
Pflaster m. (-)bandage
Pfund n. (-e) pound
Picknick n. picnic
Pille f. (-n) pill
Pilz m. (-e) mushroom
Platz m. (-e) place, seat; square
Polizei f. police; -wache f. (-n) police
    station
Polizist m. (-en) policeman
Pommes Frites pl. french fries
populär popular
Portmonnaie n. (-s) purse
Post f. post, post office; -amt n. ("er) post
    office; -answeisung f. (-en) money
    order; -beamte(r)/in m. f. (-, innen)
    post office clerk; -fach n. p.o. box;
    -karte f. (-n) post card
präsentieren present
Preis m. (-e) price; preiswert good
    value
prima! great!
prüfen check, test
Puder m. (-) powder
Pullover m. (-) sweater

Quetschung f. (-en) bruise
Quittung f. (-en) receipt

Rad n. ("er) wheel; -fahren n. cycling
Radio n. (-s) radio
Rang m. ("e) row
Rasierapparat m. (-e) razor
    Rasiercreme f. shaving cream;
    Rasierklingen pl. razor blades
raten advise
Rathaus n. ("er) town hall
Raucher m. smoker
Raum m. ("e) room

Rechner m. (-) calculator
Rechnung f. (-en) bill
recht right; rechts on the right
Regen m. rain; -mantel m. (") raincoat;
    regnen (verb) rain
Reifen m. tire; -druck m. tire pressure;
    -panne f. flat tire
Reis m. rice
Reise f. (-n) journey; -büro n. (-s) travel
    agency; -führer m. (-) guidebook;
    -scheck m. (-s) traveler's check;
    -tasche f. (-n) travel bag
Rennbahn f. (-en) race course
Rentner/in m. f. (-, innen) retiree
Reparatur f. (-en) repair; -werkstatt f.
    ("e) (repair) garage
reparieren repair
reservieren reserve; reserviert
    reserved
Restaurant n. (-s) restaurant
Rezept n. (-e) prescription
Rheinwein m. (-e) Rhine wine
richtig right
Richtung f. (-en) direction; in - in the
    direction (of)
Rindfleisch n. beef
Rock m. ("e) skirt
rosa pink
Rosé m. rosé wine
rot red; Rotwein m. red wine
Rücken m. (-) back
Rückfahrkarte f. (-n) return ticket
Rucksack m. ("e) backpack
Ruderboot n. (-e) rowboat
rufen call
Ruhetag m. day off
ruhig peaceful, quite
Ruhreier pl. scrambled eggs
Rundfahrt f. (-en) tour

Saal m. (Säle) room, hall
sagen say, tell; sag mal say, tell me
Sahne f. cream
Salat m. (-e) lettuce, salad; -gurke f. (-n)
    cucumber
Salz n. salt
Saxophonist m. saxophonist
S-Bahn f. street car system
Schachtel f. (-n) box
schade: wie - what a shame
Schalterbeamte(r)/in m. f. (-, innen)
    ticket office agent
schauen look, see
Scheck m. (-s) check; -karte f. (-n) check
    card

VOCABULARY

Scheibe *f.* **(-n)** slice
Scheinwerfer *m.* **(-)** headlight
schicken send
Schießen *n.* shooting
Schinken *m.* **(-)** ham
Schlaf *m.* sleep; **-sack** *m.* (¨e) sleeping bag; **schlafen** *(verb)* sleep
Schläger *m.* **(-)** racket
Schlagsahne *f.* whipped cream
schlank slim
schlecht bad
Schlittschuhe *pl.* skates; **Schlittschuhlaufen** *n.* skating
schließen shut, close
Schloß *n.* (¨er) castle
Schlüpfer *m.* briefs
Schlüssel *m.* **(-)** key
schmecken taste
Schmerz *m.* **(-en)** pain; **-mittel** *n.* painkiller
Schnee *m.* snow; **schneebedeckt** snow-covered; **schneien** *(verb)* snow
schnell quick(ly)
Schnitzel *n.* **(-)** cutlet
Schokolade *f.* **(-n)** chocolate
Scholle *f.* **(-n)** flounder
schon already
schön lovely, beautiful; **danke-** thanks very much; **bitte -** please, don't mention it
schrecklich dreadful
Schuh *m.* **(-e)** shoe, boot
Schuld *f.* **(-en)** fault
Schule *f.* **(-n)** school
schwanger pregnant
schwarz black; **Schwarzbrot** *m.* rye bread; **Schwarzwald** *m.* Black Forest
Schweinefleisch *n.* pork
Schwester *f.* **(-)** sister
Schwimmbad *n.* (¨er) swimming pool
schwimmen swim
See *f.* **(-n)** sea; **-m (-n)** lake; **-zunge** *f.* **(-n)** sole
sehen see, look
Sehenswürdigkeit *f.* **(-en)** sights
sehr very, very much
Seife *f.* **(-n)** soap
sein *(verb)* be; **-** *(adj.)* his, its
seit *(+ dat.)* since
Seite *f.* **(-en)** side, page
Sekretärin *f.* **(-innen)** secretary
Sekunde *f.* **(-n)** second
Selbstbedienung *f.* self-service
Semmeln *pl.* rolls

senden send
Senf *m.* mustard
Sessellift *m.* **(-e)** chairlift
sicherlich surely, of course
sie she, her, they, them
Sie you
sind: *see* **sein**
singen sing
Sitzplatz *m.* (¨e) seat (travel)
Ski *m.* **(-er)** ski; **-fahren** *n.* skiing; **-gelände** *f.* ski resort; **-lehrer** *m.* ski instructor; **-schuhe/-stiefel** *pl.* ski boots; **-stock** *m.* (¨e) ski poles
so so; **soviel** so much, many
sobald as soon as
sofort right away
Sohn *m.* (¨e) son
sollen have to, ought, should
Sommer *m.* summer
Sonne *f.* **(-n)** sun; **-nbrand** *m.* sunburn; **-nschirm** *m.* **(-e)** sunshade
sonnig sunny
sonst: -noch etwas? anything else?
Sorge: machen Sie sich keine -n don't worry
Sparkasse *f.* **(-n)** savings bank
spät late
Spaziergang *m.* (¨e) walk; **einen - machen** go for a walk
Speck *m.* bacon
Speisekarte *f.* **(-n)** menu
Speiseöl *n.* cooking oil
Speisezimmer *n.* **(-)** dining room
Spezialität *f.* **(-en)** speciality
Spiegel *m.* **(-)** mirror; **-ei** *n.* **(-er)** fried egg
Spiel *n.* **(-e)** game; **spielen** *(verb)* play
Sport *m.* sports; **-trieben** to participate in sports; **-art** *f.* **(-en)** (type of) sports; **-zentrum** *n.* **(-tren)** gym
sprechen speak
Stadion *n.* **(-ien)** stadium
Stadt *f.* (¨e) town; **-fest** *n.* **(-e)** town festival; **-mitte** *f.* town center; **-plan** *m.* (¨e) town map; **-rundfahrt** *f.* **(-en)** city tour
städtisch *(adj.)* town
stark strong
Station *f.* **(-en)** stop, station
stattfinden take place
Stimme *f.* **(-n)** voice
stimmt: das - that's right
Stock *m.* (¨e) stick; **-werk** *n.* **(-e)** story, floor

VOCABULARY

Storch m. ("e) stork
Strand m. ("e) beach
Straße f. (-n) street; **-nbahn** f. (-en) street car
Streichholz n. ("er) match
Strumpf m. ("e) stocking; **-hose** f. (-en) tights
Stück n. (-e) piece, play
Stunde f. (-n) hour; **stündlich** hourly
Sturm m. ("e) storm
suchen look for
Süd, Süden south
Super n. super (gas)
Supermarkt m. ("e) supermarket
Suppe f. (-n) soup
süß sweet
Sweatshirt n. (-s) sweatshirt

Tablette f. (-n) tablet
Tafel f. (-n) bar (chocolate)
Tag m. (-e) day; **guten -!** hello, good day!; **-esgedeck** n. today's special
täglich daily
Tal n. ("er) valley
Tankstelle f. ("e) gas station
tanzen dance
Taschenlampe f. (-n) flashlight
Tasse f. (-n) cup
Taucheranzug m. ("e) wet suit
Taxi n. (-s) taxi; **-stand** m. taxi stand
Tee m. (-s) tea
Teigwaren pl. pasta
teilnehmen take part (in)
Telefon n. (-e) telephone; **-nummer** f. (-n) telephone number; **-zelle** f. (-n) phone booth; **telefonieren** (verb) call
Telegramm n. (-e) telegram
Temperatur f. (-en) temperature
Tennis n. tennis; **-platz** m. ("e) tennis court
Termin m. (-e) appointment
Terrasse f. (-n) terrace
teuer expensive
Theater n. (-) theater
Tisch m. (-e) table
Tochter f. (-n) daughter
Toilette f. (-n) toilet
toll! great!
Tor n. (-en) arch, gate
Torte f. (-en) torte, cake
tragen wear, carry
treffen meet
Treffpunkt m. (-e) meeting place

treiben: Sport - participate in sports
Treppe f. (-n) stairs
trinken drink
trocken dry
Tschüß! good-bye! (fam.)
Tür f. (-en) door
Turnhalle f. (-n) gymnasium
Turm m. ("e) tower
typisch typical

über (+ acc./dat.) over, above
übergeben, sich vomit
Übernachtung f. (-en) **mit Frühstück** bed and breakfast
Uhr f. (-en) hour, o'clock; watch, clock
um (+ acc.) at, around, about
umsehen, sich look around
umsteigen change
Umsteigenmöglichkeit f. (-en) connecting (train)
umwechseln change
Unfall m. accident
Universität f. (-en) university
uns (acc./dat.) us, to us
unser our
unten below, at the bottom
unter (+ acc./dat.) under, below, beneath
Unterricht m. (e) lessons, instruction
unterschreiben sign
Untertiteln pl. subtitles
Urlaub m. (-e) vacation; **auf-** on vacation

Vater m. (") father; **Vati** m. Dad
verboten forbidden
verbrannt burnt
verbringen spend (time)
Vereinigten Staaten pl. USA
vergessen forget
verkaufen sell; **Verkäufer/in** m. f. (-, innen) salesclerk
Verkehr m. traffic; **-samt/sverein** n., m. ("er, -e) tourist office
verloren lost
verschieden various, different
Versicherungskosten pl. insurance costs
Verspätung f. (-en) delay; **-haben** be late
verstaucht sprained
verstehen understand
versuchen try
viel much, many

VOCABULARY

vielleicht perhaps
Viertel *n.* (-) quarter
Vollpension *f.* full board
volltanken fill it up (gas)
von *(+ dat.)* from, of
vor *(+ acc./dat.)* in front of, before
voraussichtlich prospective
vorn: nach - at the front
Vorsicht *f.* (-en) care; **vorsichtig** careful
Vorspeise *f.* (-n) hors d'œuvre, appetizer
vorstellen introduce
Vorstellung *f.* (-en) performance

waschen wash; -, **sich** wash oneself
Wagen *m.* (-) car
wählen dial
wahr: nicht -? isn't it? don't you?, etc.
während *(+ gen.)* during
Währung *f.* (-en) currency
Wald *m.* (¨e) woods, forest
Wandern *n.* hiking, walking;
  Wanderweg *m.* trail
wann when
war: *see* **sein; wäre:** *see* **sein**
warm warm, hot
warten (auf) wait (for), expect;
Wartesaal *m.* (-säle) waiting room
warum why
was what; **-für ein . . .** what a . . . , what
  sort of . . .
Wasser *n.* (-) water; **-hahn** *m.* (¨e) faucet,
  tap; **-skifahren** *n.* waterskiing
Watte *f.* cotton ball
wegen *(+ gen.)* because of, on account
  of
weh: es tut mir - it hurts (me)
Wein *m.* (-e) wine; **-karte** *f.* (-n) wine list;
  -stube (-n) wine bar; **traube** *f.* (-n)
  grape, bunch of grapes
weiß white; **Weißwein** *m.* (-e) white
  wine
weit far, distant
welcher/e/es which, what
Welt *f.* (-en) world
wer who
werden become; *(fut. tense)*
West, Westen *m.* west
Wetter *n.* weather; **-v**⟨
  weather forecast
wie how, what; **-bitte**
wieder again
Wiederhören: auf - good-bye (phone)
Wiedersehen: auf - good-bye

Wien *n.* Vienna; **wiener** Viennese
wieviel how much, many
Wind *m.* (-e) wind; **windig** windy
Winter *m.* winter; **-sport** *m.* winter
  sports
wir we
wirken work, function
wirklich really
wissen know
wo where
Woche *f.* (-n) week
woher where, from
wohin where to
wohl well
wohnen live
Wohnwagen *m.* (-) camper
Wolke *f.* (-) cloud
wollen want
wunderbar wonderful
Wunsch *m.* (¨e) wish
wünschen wish, want
würde: *see* **werden**
Wurst *f.* (¨e) sausage

zahlen pay
zählen count
Zahn *m.* (¨e) tooth; **-artz** *m.* (¨e) dentist;
  -bürste *f.* (-) toothbrush; **-pasta** *f.*
  toothpaste
zeigen show
Zeit *f.* (-en) time
Zeitung *f.* (-en) newspaper
zelten camp; **Zelt** *n.* (-e) tent; **-bett** *n.* (-)
  cot
Zimmer *n.* (-) room
Zitrone *f.* (-n) lemon
Zoll *m.* (¨e) customs
zu *(+ dat.)* to, at; too
Zucker *m.* sugar
zuerst at first
Zug *m.* (¨e) train
zum to the; **-trinken?** (what would you
  like) to drink?
zur to the
zurück back; **-fahren** go back, return;
  -gehen go back; **hin und** - round-trip

3190104668721 8

⟩r
Zuschlag *m.* surcharge
Zwiebel *f.* (-n) onion
zwischen *(+ acc./dat.)* between